Andrew Clitherow is Priest-in-Charge of St Cuthbert's Church and St John's Church in Lytham, an Honorary Canon of Blackburn Cathedral and Chaplain to the Queen. He is the author of *Into Your Hands: Prayer, and the Call to Holiness in Everyday Ministry and Life* (2001), *Renewing Faith in Ordained Ministry: New Hope for Tired Clergy* (2004), *Creative Love in Tough Times* (2007) and *Desire, Love and the Rule of St Benedict* (2008), all published by SPCK.

D1325174

PRAYER, THE EMBRACE OF LOVE

Andrew Clitherow

for my wife
Rebekah

First published in Great Britain in 2009

Society for Promoting Christian Knowledge
36 Causton Street
London SW1P 4ST

British Library Cataloguing-in-Publication Data
A catalogue record for this book is available from the British Library

ISBN 978–0–281–06152–5

1 3 5 7 9 10 8 6 4 2

Typeset by Graphicraft Limited, Hong Kong
Printed in Great Britain by Ashford Colour Press

Produced on paper from sustainable forests

Contents

Contents

Part 4
THE PRAYER OF STILLNESS

Acknowledgements

Thanks to Rebekah for her support, and to Simon, Kate, Emily and Edward for their patience.

With thanks also to Alison Barr at SPCK, and to the Revd Dr Saskia Barnden for agreeing to read the original text within a tight time-table, and for her most helpful comments and suggestions.

Introduction

This isn't the book I had planned to write. I had thought to write about prayer by exploring certain passages from the Bible. As I sat at my computer, I was surprised by the extent to which an exploration of love opened up a new appreciation of some Bible passages. So instead of writing primarily about the Bible and prayer, I have written about prayer and love.

The more I explored this theme, the more liberated I felt about the nature and purpose of prayer as I revisited some well-established interpretations of some well-known Bible passages and gained fresh insight into others. Yet somehow, through the Christian tradition, prayer has become divorced to some degree or other from love. We believe in a God of love, yet our relationship with God through prayer is often dominated by fear or a sense of duty. In a consumer-driven society, where I suspect materialism affects our faith more than we imagine, our prayers can be shaped primarily by our need to obtain the best deal for our lives and those of others.

Our prayers are very much affected by our concept of God. Even today when we say the first words of the Lord's Prayer, 'Our Father in heaven' (Matthew 6.9), we can create unhelpful images that hinder our conversation with God. To refer to God as 'Father' can somehow put him out of reach. He becomes an authoritarian figure we long to please. And whereas there will always be those who think of heaven in terms of 'up there in the clouds somewhere', for many this is a meaningless concept. So while it may have made a lot of sense for first-century Christians to pray this way, we struggle to find the same meaning in these words today. But we are mistaken if we think that Christian prayer – even in its earliest days – was shaped exclusively by a misunderstanding of the nature of God and the universe. To know God in Christ was to be caught up in the life of the universe, 'He is the image of the invisible God, the firstborn of all creation; for in him all things in heaven and on earth were created, things visible and invisible, whether thrones or dominions or rulers or powers – all things have been created through him and for him.

He himself is before all things, and in him all things hold together' (Colossians 1.15–17). Moreover, the nature of this creative energy is love. St Paul prays for other Christians that 'Christ may dwell in your hearts through faith, as you are being rooted and grounded in love' (Ephesians 3.17). It is by this love that we become at one with ourselves and others and with God (1 John 4.7–13). The language of prayer, therefore, is the language of love. Prayer is grounded in heartfelt communion with the source of creative love in the universe. Without this appreciation of love, the rhymes and rote of much formal liturgy today, and even personal prayers, can be pretty lifeless. For our communion with God is defined by radical love rather than religious respectability.

Prayer is a fundamental part of our faith. It informs us daily of our divine potential in our relationship with God, and transforms our life. At a time when many struggle to discover this love in the Church, when the foundations of society have been found to be more fragile than we ever imagined and when the future of the planet is under threat along with the well-being of billions of human beings, we have the opportunity and the responsibility to rediscover that language of love that unites earth with heaven. To do so is to 'not pull Christ toward us from heaven by prayer. Rather, we discover him within ourselves'.[1]

As we pursue this understanding of prayer as the language of love, we are led beyond mere words to a way of being where we increasingly receive and respond to divine love without hindrance. Here we are able to stand naked before God in the original simplicity of Adam and Eve. Unrestricted by ambition, misunderstanding or unhelpful religion, human and divine spirit meet in naked embrace. For those who prefer the security of predictable behaviour and clearly defined roles, this is not a safe place to pray. But it is perhaps the only way to pray if we are to immerse ourselves in the life of love. Here the greatest obstacle to prayer is our inability to love – or to engage in the processes of love – rather than our inability to lead a faultless life or master a particular mantra. Praying – like loving – is about the way we celebrate life through dynamics of heartfelt relationships that are likely to change and develop from time to time. Here we are led – often through unlikely ways and unexpected events – to a deepening appreciation of identity, meaning, fulfilment and destiny. By this prayer, we enjoy the embrace of naked love through which our senses are sharpened to the divine possibilities in daily life and the redemption of the world.

The book is divided into four sections. The first, 'Grounded through prayer', looks at the basis of prayer for the individual while the second, 'Growing through prayer', explores ways in which we might develop our prayer lives. The third section, 'Giving through prayer', looks beyond our personal needs to ways in which we might bring our prayers to bear on the life of the world for the good of all. At the end of these chapters are suggestions for 'Grounding' (doing something connected with what has gone before), together with 'Reflecting' (spending time thinking about the deeper meaning of a Bible passage) and 'Praying' (using a particular prayer in line with the theme of the chapter). Finally, the Prayer of Stillness in the fourth section provides a structure for prayer based on the use of Bible passages and the imagination. Again, this is nothing new, but is a way of prayer I have put together myself which I have found effective in the expression of the embrace of naked love. Some may find it helpful, others will not. It is offered as a way to engage the body, mind and spirit in a unity of prayer that takes us into the presence of Christ.

This was written not on a secluded island of holy isolation, but in the midst of a busy family and hectic parish life, often accompanied by telephone calls, visitors at the door and builders working on the house. It is offered in the hope of supporting the prayers of those who live, work and pray in similarly busy lives.

Andrew Clitherow
Lytham

Part 1

GROUNDED THROUGH PRAYER

1

Prayer and myself

Sacrifice and offering you do not desire, but you have given me an open ear. Burnt-offering and sin-offering you have not required. Then I said, 'Here I am; in the scroll of the book it is written of me. I delight to do your will, O my God; your law is within my heart.'
(*Psalm 40.6–8*)

A conversation initiated by God

I was told the following story the other day: a man goes to see his doctor to express his concern about his wife's hearing. While she doesn't think there is a problem, he is sure she is going deaf. But he cannot persuade her to visit the doctor to see if anything can be done to help her. The doctor suggests the man goes home and stands ten feet away from his wife and says, 'Darling, I think you have a problem with your hearing. Will you please make an appointment with the doctor and have a hearing test?' The doctor tells him that if she doesn't reply, he should repeat these words at eight, six, four and two feet distance from his wife. If his wife has not responded by the final message, the husband can use this as evidence that would perhaps convince her to visit her GP. So the husband goes home and does as the doctor has suggested. He waits for a time when the radio and television are turned off and everything in the house is quiet. He then says his prepared statement at ten, eight, six, four and two feet away from his wife. Having heard no response at all, he stands as close to her as possible and delivers the sentence for a final time. At this point, his wife looks up from her newspaper and says, 'I've already told you five times, there is nothing wrong with my hearing.'

The husband had assumed his wife's lack of response meant that there was something wrong with her. He hadn't lost the power of speech but he had unwittingly lost the ability to listen. It was only through the intervention of a third party that he discovered it was he – and not his wife – who was hard of hearing.

One definition of individual prayer is that it is a conversation between the Spirit of God and our human spirit. It has been initiated by God, who hopes we will respond. God speaks to us in many ways – through events, individuals, creation, books, articles, reading the Bible and so on. When we begin to think about prayer and to explore ways of praying, we are doing so not because we thought it would be a good idea to catch his attention and talk with God but because we are responding to something that God has 'said' to us that we have 'heard'. We are reacting to his revelation of himself. There is no need to try to make God aware of us, as he is already more aware of us than we are of ourselves. Instead, something or somebody has made us recognize the voice of God in our lives, and we have decided to respond. At this point we allow our spirit to interact with the Spirit of God in such a way that makes a prayerful conversation with him possible. At first we babble like children learning how to speak, and then we move on to converse coherently. Finally, if we make a priority of this kind of prayer, we find that the intimate prayer of the Spirit goes beyond mere words and human expressions.

Inspired by God

Just before his arrest and trial, Jesus prayed for help in the Garden of Gethsemane. In Mark's record of the prayer, Jesus addresses God as 'Abba, Father' (Mark 14.36). This is an even more familiar form of address than Matthew and Luke give us in their separate versions of the Lord's Prayer, each of which begins with 'Our Father/Father' (Matthew 6.9; Luke 11.2). While 'Father' is a more formal form of address, the meaning of 'Abba, Father' can best be expressed as 'Daddy'. But Jesus was not the only one inspired to use this intimate form of address in prayer. Writing around the same time as Mark, or maybe even a little earlier, Paul assures the Christians in Rome that when they say 'Abba! Father!' this is not because they have inspired themselves to say these words which signify their adoption as children of God (Romans 8.15). It is rather because the Spirit of God is bearing witness within them, inspiring them particularly when they feel their lives are under threat.

Paul is making an extraordinary claim at a time when Christian faith was at its most raw and in its earliest stages of formation. In the days when there were few books and you learned by listening and remembering what others said to you, the followers of Christ were being told that they could be led into the deepest possible relationship with God by allowing his Spirit the opportunity to draw them into his presence.

These early Christians travelled light. They didn't have Bibles or commentaries or spiritual masterpieces on their bookshelves at home to which they could refer. There were no helpful collections of illustrated prayers through which their hearts might be opened to heaven. But they knew that if they let him, God would inspire them with his Spirit and fill their hearts with his love. The emphasis wasn't so much on what they had to do for God but on what God could do for them.

This was not a new idea. The author of the Psalm which opens this chapter echoed these sentiments, as did some of the prophets of the Hebrew Scriptures. The verses from Psalm 40 are radical for their time in that they proclaim there is no longer any need to offer sacrifices to God in order to appease him, or to make some invest-ment in his goodwill for the future, or to be acceptable to him. Instead, the author encourages his readers to understand the importance of saying to God in prayer, 'Here I am'. Having said this, they had to be prepared to listen to him, and follow his will for their lives in a heartfelt kind of way rather than for personal or religious gain. These inspired words of the psalmist find their fulfilment hundreds of years later in the life and witness of Jesus Christ.

Here I am

Sometimes when we pray we forget to say, 'Here I am'. This may be because the way we pray has become affected by the way we live. While there are those who cannot cope with being still and silent, and while some prayers have to be said 'on the move', most of us need occasions when we can simply – in silence, and without dis-traction – spend some time with God. Then we begin by saying 'Here I am', and sometimes it is all we need to say. It is particularly at times such as this, when we are prepared to be vulnerable in God's presence, that his Spirit inspires us to call him 'Daddy' and we become enveloped by his love.

When our prayers are not so much about 'Here I am', they can be about 'Here they are'. A 'Here they are' approach to prayer consists primarily of masses of statements, requests and observations that represent all the things that are on our minds at the time. 'Here they are' or 'Here they come, God, all the neuroses of my life. Stand by for a near-suffocating avalanche of stress-related prayer!' 'Here they are' prayers often reflect our longing for God to become more involved in our life, while revealing how far away from God and how restless our hearts have become. We think we are pouring out our hearts to God by telling him what to do with his world and the people who make life impossible for us ('What are you going to do about this?'). We assume that simply by saying prayers, going to church or giving to those in need, we are justified in his sight, while our hearts may actually be full of hatred rather than love ('Just admire my faith and love'). And we feel isolated and alone a lot of the time ('I admit it, my heart has gone cold'). The psalmist, on the other hand, knows that religion only makes sense when, without conditions, we place ourselves in God's hands ('Here I am'). Here we can build a relationship based on faith and love ('I delight to do your will') which is grounded in a deep spiritual communion between ourselves and God ('Your law is written in my heart').

If prayer is a heartfelt way of communication, it is natural that from time to time we might feel the need to pour out our hearts to God. But when we fill the available time – which may be very precious in a busy life – with such words as these and these alone, we may end up wondering whether God can hear us. Yet, like the man in the story at the beginning of the chapter, it is we who have become hard of hearing, not God. What is more, our prayers are now less likely to have been empowered by the Spirit who has been crowded out by the host of our concerns. Particularly on those occasions when we want to unburden ourselves – although it is by no means necessary to do this every time we pray – having poured out our hearts to God, we have to allow the time and space for him to pour the Spirit of his love into us. We do not need to justify our existence or win favour with God by giving airtime to endless words and concerns. His love is unconditional. Rather than grasping or grovelling our way into God's presence, all we need do is put ourselves in the Way of his love by saying, 'Here I am'. When we say this, rather than concentrating on ourselves, we are making room for Christ to be at the heart of our praying.

As we learn how to pray this way, we say in our minds or out loud 'Here I am' maybe as we begin our prayers. We may also at the same time want to ask the Holy Spirit to inspire us in our prayers so that we can make the most of the divine energies in and around us. The psalmist doesn't write that we have grown our ears ourselves in order to listen to God. Our ears are a gift from God so that we can listen to him. Some translations at this point have, 'Ears you have dug for me'. Again we are reminded that we don't have to earn the right to pray and hear the voice of God. He has already given us all we need in order to engage in faithful praying. Jesus' final promise to those who would follow him was, 'And remember, I am with you always, to the end of the age' (Matthew 28.20). As we become increasingly aware of his presence, we concentrate on being present to God in that place where Spirit and love become not only the channel but also the essence of our communication.

Beginning with ourselves

We often think that prayer is first and foremost about God. While in many ways this is true, prayer has first and foremost to begin with ourselves. This is because while God can be described as being 'above and beyond' us, he is also alongside and within. As God became incarnate ('en-fleshed') in Jesus, by his Spirit he seeks to become increasingly alive in us. And divine Spirit particularly combines with human spirit whenever we make room for this to occur within ourselves. 'Here I am' means 'I am not trying to be or do anything other than be open to you. Free of any need for self-justification or ingratiation, I offer you myself as a temple in which I invite you to dwell'. As we learn to pray more and more like this, the Spirit of God and the spirit of ourselves combine so that it becomes increasingly difficult to separate God in Christ from ourselves. At some stage as we progress in this way of prayer, we will discover that we are no longer beginning our prayers by saying in our minds or out loud, 'Here I am'. Instead we discover these words have moved from our minds and mouths and are now being 'spoken' in the depths of our hearts – and at the same time in the heart of God.

The man in the story at the beginning of the chapter thought effective communication depended completely on his wife listening to what he had to say. If we begin to pray with our focus entirely on God, we can become so caught up in the need to relate to the One who is 'above and beyond' that we think prayer depends upon persuading God to listen to what we have to say. Before long, *we* who are deaf proclaim that *God* is deaf or worse. We become frustrated at his lack of concern. We try to talk to him, but he doesn't listen. We drift apart.

Prayer has to be first of all about our awareness of ourselves, before it can be about our faith in God. Our praying benefits enormously when we can say, 'Here I am' in such a way that we begin to make useful connections between ourselves and the One who creates and sustains the universe through Jesus Christ. (We will look at this in a little more detail in the next chapter.) Again, this is nothing new in the history of Christian prayer, 'The ladder of the kingdom is hidden within you, within your soul. Dive down into yourself, away from sin, and there you will find the ladder by which you can ascend.'[2]

Finally we note that the psalmist reminds us that instead of engaging in meaningless rituals, we should concentrate on having our 'ears open to God'. As we have seen, this involves the willingness and ability to listen carefully. We cannot underestimate the importance of this holy listening. Without it we cannot obey God, nor can we follow the Way of Jesus Christ. In the New Testament the word most commonly used for 'obey' means literally 'listen'. We cannot obey if we are not prepared to listen. If we do not listen, we cannot obey. 'But not all have obeyed the good news;' writes St Paul, 'for Isaiah says, "Lord, who has believed our message?" So faith comes from what is heard, and what is heard comes through the word of Christ' (Romans 10.16–17).

So, in the Christ-centred self, it is the ability to say 'Here I am' in a way that at the same time opens us to our deepest selves and to God that leads us to a prayer-filled life.

Grounding

Ask yourself how much of your praying is about saying to God, 'Here I am'. Is there any way in which you could usefully incorporate this into your existing prayer life or into any new forms of praying you would like to follow? Try to find some quality time and a place where you can relax and be still in the presence of God and pray silently, 'Here I am'. You can say this once or repeat it as often as is helpful. As you do this, you might like to focus on a picture of Jesus, or an object such as a lit candle, to help you address this prayer to the living God. Each time you say these words, imagine the 'Here you are' things you bring to prayer falling away from you. Let go of things such as your desire to tell God what to do about the world, your fears and prejudices, your plans and schemes for which you seek his approval, and so on. Eventually, you will reach that place where the 'Here you are' things have all gone and all that is left is the vulnerable, naked you saying simply, 'Here I am'. When you have reached this point, it is important that you stay in this silent vulnerability. In this quiet emptiness the divine Spirit will speak to your spirit. Listen gently, therefore, for as long as is appropriate. Try not to listen too hard otherwise this just becomes another 'Here they are' prayer as you try to force God to speak to you. When we listen gently, we can become aware of the Word that is in our hearts speaking gently to us. Conclude this time of prayer by saying the Lord's Prayer, or any suitable prayer of your own, or a favourite that someone else has written. Write down any thoughts that have come to you in the stillness of this prayer (you might have made a note of them earlier as and when they came to you). Decide to come back to these thoughts later on and maybe turn them over in your mind so that you can understand them and make the most of them for your life. If this has been helpful, work out another time and place when you can return to God again to say, 'Here I am'.

Next time you go to a service in church, try going a little earlier to spend some quiet time saying, 'Here I am', so that when the time of worship begins, you are in the right place with God in order to give and receive.

Reflecting

Now there was a disciple in Damascus named Ananias. The Lord said to him in a vision, 'Ananias.' He answered, 'Here I am, Lord.'

(Acts 9.10)

The Lord clearly knew where Ananias was, so this reply is to be understood in terms of his openness to God and willingness to do his will. In the verses that follow, we read how Ananias was called to lead Saul to faith in Jesus Christ. Saul subsequently became the apostle to the Gentile world.

Praying

Here I am, Lord.
Draw me into your presence,
envelop me with your love
that by deep communion
Spirit and truth
will set me free
to be who I am,
Lord. Amen.

2

Prayer and joy

'My soul magnifies the Lord, and my spirit rejoices in God my Saviour, for he has looked with favour on the lowliness of his servant. Surely, from now on all generations will call me blessed; for the Mighty One has done great things for me, and holy is his name.'
(*Luke 1.46–49*)

Joy and faith

While most of us experience joy from time to time, few of us can be joyful all the time. So we need to be confident that we can be Christians who are full of joy at the deepest level without necessarily expressing or feeling this at an emotional level all the time.

While we may have a deep sense of joy in our believing (Romans 15.13), as followers of Jesus Christ today, we will not necessarily feel happy all the time. Prayerful joy is a by-product of faith. It is very deep and profound. But prayerful joy is not simply the result of our complete assurance that we have all the answers, or because, at any point of time, everything seems to be going well for us. While it is highly likely that Jesus was a joyful person (Luke 15.7), we are also told that Jesus wept over Jerusalem (Luke 19.41) and the death of a friend (John 11.35) and that he became frustrated and fed up at times, not least with his closest friends (Mark 9.19). There are those who have been blessed with a permanent, sunny and positive disposition. I remember a fellow ordinand at theological college many years ago who was constantly happy. Every time he emerged from his room, he would be singing or whistling. You could hear him throughout the college. He would even sing on his way to the laundry. At one level, he was the most joyous Christian I have ever known. When I was feeling good, he was a joy to be with. When I was feeling down, his constant chirpiness used to drive me nuts, for *I* have not been blessed with a constantly sunny disposition. For me, and I suspect for many others, the highs and lows of life can fill us with great joy but can also leave us feeling grim. For us, joy is something we express through our emotions at particular times, but it is also and especially a treasure held within our hearts which we frequently forget or fail to give expression to. On occasions, I wonder if my faith has made any difference to the way I live my life. I don't always have the peace beyond all understanding that Paul talks about (Philippians 4.7). But when I consider what I would be like without my faith, I realize how much worse things could be. So joy becomes especially present sometimes when we realize how much our spirits have become closer to the Spirit of God.

So there is the joy that we feel when things go right, such as when we have a sense that our prayers have been answered. And there is an even deeper spiritual joy that lies at the heart of the believer even though it may not be apparent for much – or even most – of the time. As it lies deep within us, we sometimes have to search for it beneath emotions that can be affected in any number of ways on any day of the week. The most effective way to reach these depths of spirit is by prayer.

Prayerful joy that comes in times of questioning or when our faith is weak arises from that place within us where human spirit searches for divine Spirit. Our prayerful awareness of Jesus Christ both in good and in difficult times is a source of constant joy in the believer. Following the ascension of Jesus, Luke tells us that the disciples 'worshipped him, and returned to Jerusalem with great joy; and they were continually in the temple blessing God' (Luke 24.52–53). But the disciples were joyful also when they were not very sure about what was going on. Just prior to the verse above, Luke describes how they were full of joy even before they fully accepted they were living in the presence of Jesus, 'While in their joy they were disbelieving' (Luke 24.41). This reminds us that the joy of the Christian life is not always the result of a complete assurance of the presence of Christ with us. We can be joyful even when we are not sure, when there are more questions than answers and straightforward faith is not possible.

We are blessed by being able to ask our questions and share our problems prayerfully in the company of Jesus, at the foot of the cross or on the mount of the Beatitudes, in the synagogue at Capernaum, on the Sea of Galilee, in the Temple in Jerusalem and so on. From time to time, we may experience a kind of ecstasy when life, the world, the universe and God fit together and make sense, providing us with a feeling of meaning, purpose and peace. This, we may imagine, is how Mary felt when she heard the greeting of her cousin Elizabeth whereby her faith and understanding were confirmed. Mary sings her song of joy (to which we shall come later) not because of what she had achieved but because of what God had done for her. This in itself can be a pattern for all our similar celebrations lest we should become so filled with pride that we think we are solely responsible for the good times we enjoy.

The prayerful joy of the heart can also arise out of the sometimes arid soil of prayerful questioning and reflection. We need to remind ourselves of this from time to time so that we can appreciate and treasure these occasions as much as the times of divine disclosure. We may be familiar with the idea that difficult times in faith are often those occasions when, if we remain positive, we learn the most significant lessons about ourselves and our relationship with God. This process is rarely straightforward and often we only understand how we have grown in faith as we look back on dark times when prayer was difficult or impossible. But for those who understand and can keep in touch with that prayerful joy that arises out of our faithful memory of God's action in our lives, there is a celebration of faith to be had even when we may be struggling to make sense of what is going on. Unfortunately, we tend to equate a sense of the absence of God with some measure of personal failure which robs us of this faithful joy. It is likely that Mary will also have had times when her joy will have come from heartfelt faith rather than present experience, such as at the wedding in Cana of Galilee (John 2.1–11) and when it may have appeared that Jesus was redefining his family relationships (Matthew 12.46–50).

In a troubled world, the Christian faith is a source of joy even and especially in the difficult times (Galatians 5.22). This joy may well make us feel good from time to time but if it doesn't, we should not assume it to be absent. For joy is not only expressed in the laughter of the Spirit but also in the heart that trusts in the God who, as we saw in the previous chapter, is forever calling us to draw closer to him in ever-deepening love. And this joy in believing is never more evident than when we pray, 'You show me the path of life. In your presence there is fullness of joy; in your right hand are pleasures for evermore' (Psalm 16.11).

We may not feel that our faith provides us with 'answers' to all of life's problems so as to give us an experience of joy in all circumstances. It may well, however, provide us with the Way to learn and relearn our identity and the purpose of our lives as we grow closer to God. Here our faith is a source of joy because it helps us respond to the divine love that lies at the heart of the universe so that we may live fully in a world where little is assured.

Joy and thankfulness

Joy in prayer arises out of a thankful heart for all that God has done – and continues to do – for us. Mary's song, or the Magnificat as it is generally known, is a most powerful example of this. As we read or pray the Magnificat for ourselves, we remember how Mary visits Elizabeth, her cousin, who is soon to give birth to John the Baptist, the forerunner of Christ. And it is at this meeting, following the acclamation of Elizabeth, that Luke gives expression to Mary's joy in the hymn that has become central to the prayer of the Church and has been said every day as part of the Evening Office for hundreds of years.

Mary's soul becomes great in her worship of God – she makes even greater the presence of God within her innermost being – because of her joy in believing. This joy has come to her because, despite her humble position in society and in the religious institutions of her time, she has come to know God as her saviour. As a result of her cousin's confirmation of all that God has done for her, Mary is joyful in spirit. In magnifying God, Mary refers to him as the Mighty One who has done great things for her. As a result of her joy and gratitude for the way in which God has conceived his son in her womb, she acknowledges that God is even greater than she had previously thought. 'If God has chosen me for this, then how great must he be.'

While Mary's story is unique in the history of the Church, her song is very similar to Hannah's song of praise when she, many years earlier, rejoices that God has granted her a son, Samuel, whom she dedicates to God's service. Until that time she had thought she was barren (1 Samuel 2.1–10). Here again, in a different setting, joy in prayer comes as an expression of thanksgiving for all that God has done. So we are left with a sense that all prayer should include an expression of joyful thanksgiving. For we also need to give thanks for the ways in which we feel God has saved us and brought about new life within us, not only for our own benefit but also for the good of others.

I suspect that if we did not live in such a rush, we would have more time to appreciate the joy in the gift of each new day. We would also have time to express the joy God gives us by means of our most significant relationships where, through love, we are drawn into the mystery of life. We would also have more joy in the gift of family life. Sometimes our prayers lack joy and gratitude because they are not grounded in our daily lives.

When we do not pray with joyful and thankful hearts and minds, it is sometimes because we have forgotten all that God has done for us. Or we may have fallen into a state of ingratitude by taking things for granted. While we may not always feel a sense of joy, we need to remind ourselves from time to time that God who lived in Mary's soul and spirit, also longs to live in us. Sometimes, however, it takes someone else to point out to us how blessed we are, as Elizabeth did for Mary. And there is no reason why, just as God blessed Hannah, he will not also bless our lives, barren sometimes of the things we most long for. Prayer without joy can be prayer without faith. When we do not experience joy, it is sometimes because we refuse to accept what we have already been given. We consider what we have as not enough, or the gifts and blessings that we are aware of as inferior to the ones we would really like to possess. But our experience of prayer should not depend upon whether we have or have not received what we regard as necessary. Otherwise, like spoilt children, we will be joyful when we have our own way and miserable when we don't. By contrast, through authentic prayer we can receive either the granting of our requests, or the faith and understanding we require to turn our disappointments into sources of joy. 'Ask and you will receive, so that your joy may be complete,' says Jesus (John 16.24). This is so because we ask according to the name of Jesus – we magnify his name – so that whatever the outcome, by praying in this way we receive increasingly the spirit and life of Jesus. Here our joy comes from our relationship with Jesus together with the love of God we have known through him in the past.

Joy and myself

We saw in the first chapter how God calls to us from the depths of ourselves and it is the discovery of our personal relationship with God that enables this joy to well up within us. 'I AM' was the name through which God revealed himself to Moses in the burning bush (Exodus 3.14).[3] In the life of Jesus, especially in the record of the Fourth Gospel, we see how we may find our destiny fulfilled by the fullness of God in Jesus who said, 'I am the way, and the truth and the life' (John 14.6). As we seek to follow Jesus we are called to know that being human is about becoming the 'I am' through which God calls us to share in the divinity of Christ. Our re-creation begins with our recognition of the way in which we have all been called to bear God to the world. Even the most committed sometimes need to be reminded of this, particularly when their prayers have grown cold. 'I suddenly discovered Him in me under the name "I AM". That was my turning-point: I perceived Being in a different perspective, the opposite of the way I had seen things before this blessed miracle.'[4] There can be no greater source of joy in the spirit than to have faith in who 'I am' and to know that we, too, can be 'filled with all the fullness of God' (Ephesians 3.19) so that 'our spirit, regenerated by prayer, begins to marvel at the sublime mystery of being.'[5]

Grounding

St Paul encourages the people who lived in Thessalonica to 'Rejoice always, pray without ceasing', and to 'give thanks in all circumstances; for this is the will of God in Christ Jesus for you' (1 Thessalonians 5.18). So, joy inspired by thanksgiving is an essential part of our daily prayers not least because it is an expression of our recognition of how much God has done for us. To speak to God in prayer in terms of joy and thanksgiving – regardless of how we might be feeling – is to divert attention away from ourselves and onto God. It is good, therefore, to begin our prayers in this way.

Even if joy and thanksgiving form a part of your prayer life, take a moment to stop and make a list of all the things God has done for you – and for others – that give you a sense of joy and celebration. Some things may come to you straightaway but you may be surprised by how much more there is if you set aside a little time to remember it all.

When you have completed your list, try and devise a way in which you express your joy in prayer and worship, so that you may make even more room for him to be the God who does great things for you and whose name is holy. If you don't do so already, you may wish to incorporate Mary's song (the Magnificat) into your evening prayers.

Reflecting

For this reason I bow my knees before the Father, from whom every family in heaven and on earth takes its name. I pray that, according to the riches of his glory, he may grant that you may be strengthened in your inner being with power through his Spirit, and that Christ may dwell in your hearts through faith, as you are being rooted and grounded in love. I pray that you may have the power to comprehend, with all the saints, what is the breadth and length and height and depth, and to know the love of Christ that surpasses knowledge, so that you may be filled with all the fullness of God.   (Ephesians 3.14–19)

Praying

God grant me a joyful heart
in thanksgiving
for all he has done for me,
for all that I am
and by the Spirit of Christ,
for all that I hope to be.
Amen.

3

Prayer and sin

━━━◆◆◆━━━

And the LORD *God commanded the man, 'You may freely eat of every tree of the garden; but of the tree of the knowledge of good and evil you shall not eat, for in the day that you eat of it you shall die.'*
(*Genesis 2.16–17*)

All that I have I give to you

To conduct a marriage service is an enormous privilege. Many parish clergy consider it to be one of the most enjoyable aspects of their ministry. I can remember the first one I took. I wasn't expecting to be more nervous than the bride and groom. Looking back on it, I think I must have closely resembled Rowan Atkinson's portrayal of the green young clergyman in the film *Four Weddings and a Funeral* (although I don't think I said 'Holy Goat' instead of Holy Ghost!).

Sometimes it is at the rehearsal a few nights before the service itself that the unexpected happens. Recently, although her groom was to give her a ring, the bride-to-be asked me if she could give her husband a wrist watch in the service as he never wore a ring for health and safety reasons related to his work. At another rehearsal of the marriage of two lawyers who were clearly very much in love, there was an unexpected pause when they came to say the words that accompany the giving of the rings. All was going well until we came to the words, 'all that I am I give to you, and all that I have I share with you'. At this point both lawyers drew a sharp intake of breath. I didn't ask whether these words contravened any pre-nuptial agreement they had made but from the look on their faces, they may well have. I was relieved when, following a brief conversation, they agreed to say them. And as far as I know the couple have lived happily and together ever after.

The two lawyers knew, of course, that the love that two people have for each other that leads them to make a lifelong commitment

19

is not conditional. It is not a question of one person loving another so long as he gives up watching football on Saturdays or she promises sometimes to unhook her mobile from her ear, or gives up watching soaps on television, or he has nothing ever to do with his overbearing parents in the future. Nor is it a question of keeping to ourselves those aspects of our personalities we would rather not share because we are too embarrassed about them or consider them too problematic. Most people bring some kind of emotional baggage to a lifelong relationship, and when we commit ourselves to someone else, we agree to share our joys and bear our burdens together.

Unconditional love that forms the basis of a lifelong partnership involves mutual self-disclosure and self-offering. We agree to this because while we can achieve fulfilment and happiness on our own, we know that only together can we discover more fully the purpose of our lives and therein the fulfilment of our love.

The gift of love

To be able to celebrate this degree of love for someone else – together with their love for us – is one of the most precious gifts we can be given. We become conscious again that life itself – every day – is a gift to be cherished and treasured. We are aware that we did not earn the life we have or the love that we give or receive. And for most people in long-term relationships, and also those who love yet live on their own, there is always more to learn. For in committed relationships we tend to learn about love as we go along, rather than knowing all the answers to begin with. And this can be exciting, invigorating, challenging and downright scary at times.

When, however, we wrongly assume that such love is our right rather than a gift, things can go wrong. In the *Common Worship* marriage service, the bride and groom agree to 'love and cherish' one another, but we cannot cherish someone we regard as a possession whose love we have earned. Difficulties arise in relationships whether we are married or single, when we take love for granted rather than as a gift, when we demand things from others simply because we consider them to be our rights. Even today, I suppose, we might regard it as our right to have a cooked breakfast every day, or that our partner should do the housekeeping or shopping or take sole responsibility for bringing up the children, or that it is our right to take holidays abroad whenever we want, or have sex on demand.

There is, of course, no argument to be had when both partners have agreed to any of these so-called rights as the way they want to run their lives. But when we decide unilaterally that we have rights we expect to be observed at all times by our partner, it may be that we have begun to care less for the integrity of the other and now regard the partnership more in terms of selfish need, rather than as the joint venture it once was. Left unchecked, this desire to organize our own lives independently of our spouses and partners to whom we have committed ourselves can lead to the disintegration of the love that was both the power and purpose of our shared life in the first place. Consequently, not only is the relationship in the present damaged, sometimes irrevocably, but the future, that once beckoned with promise of new life, identity and a destiny that reached even beyond the horizon of our dreams, is also lost.

The importance of staying close

So what has all this to do with prayer and sin? When some Christians speak about sin, they emphasize specific acts that reveal our less-than-perfect behaviour. To behave in a sinful way is to do something that isn't helpful or respectable, or that hurts others. But sin is not primarily about whether we are dismissive of others, lie or indulge in sharp business practices, for example. While we could describe these as godless acts, sin primarily refers to the way we have a habit of putting a distance between ourselves and God. While the act of ignoring someone else's need may be described as sinful, the sin that causes this is the underlying attitude we have that others don't matter. Or if we refuse to apologize to someone we have offended, or refuse to at least attempt to forgive someone who has caused us pain, the sin is not so much in our silence or lack of communication but in our underlying conviction that we are always right and can live happily on our own. There is another way to live rather than the way that isolates us from others, ourselves and even God. It is not easy, but we are more likely to find our own healing and fulfilment this way. For when we pursue the way of love, we come close to God, whereas when we pursue the way of sin, God becomes an alien being and we end up in a meaningless environment. So where we are in relation to God and others usually determines whether we behave in a sinful or godly way. In this sense, we all have to choose either to live in relation to God or on our own.

21

More fundamentally, we have to choose whether we regard life as a gift to be cherished with others or as a right to be used for ourselves alone.

The story of Adam and Eve is about the consequences of the choices we make in the way we live our lives. This symbolic story, written perhaps during the reign of King Solomon in the tenth century BC, describes how human beings find themselves at a distance from God because they have decided to regard their lives in terms of rights rather than gift. Here they prefer to use creation for their own ends rather than in partnership with the one who gave them life in the first place. So the consequences of this sin are that we fail to fulfil our God-given potential. As we fall short of the glory of God that we are supposed to enjoy (Romans 3.23), we find ourselves in godless places because we have chosen to ignore love at the expense of selfish ambition. The way back is to be found by the grace of God, and prayer is the primary channel of that grace.

This is where the marriage analogy can be helpful. For our relationship with God is founded on unconditional love and lifelong commitment. In fact, the Church has often been described as the bride of Christ. So where we are with God at any stage of our life of faith can be likened to where we are in a long-term committed relationship of love. There are times when we cherish our knowledge of God, and regard both our life and the love we have as gifts that bring the glory of God into the present. As a result we can feel very close to God, in love with him, and we rejoice in his abundant life. And then there are times when we decide to grab the gift of life and live it primarily for ourselves. Cherishing a gift is all right until it gets in the way of what we want to do. Love, like prayer, can be tiresome. It takes too much time in a busy life and we become frustrated by the way both love and prayer demand that we constantly develop our self-awareness. We convince ourselves that we don't understand God at all or that he doesn't understand us. We grow tired of our relationship and decide to do our own thing, possibly with someone else.

Holding on to the gift

All sinful behaviour has its origin in the sin of putting ourselves at a distance from God, just as loveless behaviour towards other human beings comes from putting a distance between ourselves and them. So the greatest obstacle we can put between ourselves and God is referred to by Jesus as the sin against the Holy Spirit (Matthew 12.31–32). Here we understand the Holy Spirit to be God's energy of love that redeems the world. What Jesus seems to be saying is that while we can have our problems and disagreements with him – we might complain about him, lose our temper with him, shout at him – we can still remain in love with him. But when we walk away from him, we cut ourselves off from the life we are meant to share with him and the gifts he wants to share with us. The unconditional love of God never fails. It is always there, beckoning, healing, restoring. But from time to time we decide we don't want it. And then we discover that to cut ourselves off from love is the greatest mistake we can make. It is like turning our back on our spouse, partner or close friends. As we concentrate on what we believe is rightfully ours, we ignore the fact that honouring our vows, keeping to the agreement, hanging in there, sometimes against our will, costs. For – as in the story of Adam and Eve – costly love brings us to life whereas arrogance kills us. Divine love leads us to eternity whereas pride can take us to the hell of unredeemed human ambition.

Sometimes we become afraid that God wants to take over our lives. We are afraid to pray more than we do because we are afraid he will keep us in the place where we cannot be ourselves. He will take away our sense of fun and turn us into boring introverts. But his love does not work like this. Far from it. For we believe that when our lives are blessed by the love of God, we can enjoy ourselves even more while taking full responsibility for how we live. We believe that God has a purpose for our lives and he calls us to find out what that purpose is and to live in harmony with it. Returning to the marriage service, the minister says about the bride and groom, 'Therefore, on this their wedding day we pray with them, that, strengthened and guided by God, they may fulfil his purpose for the whole of their earthly life together'.[6] In a similar way, God doesn't call any of us to live in isolation from him, but to be with him as he is with us. Here we can make sense of our love and this life whether we are in long-term committed relationships or not.

So when as a result of sin we find that we have put ourselves beyond the love of God, we also know that as a result of our continued commitment we can discover that we are enveloped by his love. And prayer is essentially – that is, by its very essence – the dialogue of that love between God and ourselves and ourselves and

God. Prayer involves all our emotions. We give thanks in prayer and we celebrate life in prayer. We also cry and stamp our feet in prayer. But both feeling good and feeling frustrated are part of love. And when we have spent our energies in exuberance or pain, we rest exhausted in the divine embrace. It is vital, therefore, that we are aware of the nature of sin and its consequences for our prayers if our love is to be fruitful.

Great emphasis is often placed on the need for us to confess our sins before and during prayer so that our conversation with God can be as free of misunderstanding as possible. In the same way, our conversations with our friends and families are more straightforward and effective if we are not harbouring some resentment or difficult secret in our hearts. But first and foremost our conversations with those closest to ourselves are most helpful when they are grounded in love, when we remember that our love is a gift and not our right. In the same way, when we pray, we need to be aware of the place from which we are praying, where our hearts are in relation to the heart of God. Our awareness of our sinfulness in this regard is central to the effectiveness of our prayers or prayer time. For the unconditional love of God, such as we come across in Scripture, in which we are called to share is also sacramental. In other words, through this language of prayer God comes to life in us as his Spirit and our spirits become one. So if we have – consciously or unconsciously – made a vow of love to God and accepted his commitment to us, we need to ask ourselves when we pray how much we are living within the garden of his life or outside it. How much are we living life as a gift or as a right? Sometimes when life becomes really challenging or maybe when we have simply been lazy, we can suddenly discover that we are outside the garden and have quenched the flow of life with which the Spirit seeks to fill us.

I don't know how true it is but I once heard a story of an occasion when a bishop on a remote island in the southern hemisphere at the beginning of a service, dressed in cope and mitre, processed into a cathedral where the walls consisted of rushes and grass. He made his way up the aisle and into the sanctuary during the opening hymn and sat on the episcopal throne that had been put in place especially for him. He sat down and as he leant back in his seat, it toppled over. He fell through the flimsy wall behind him and suddenly discovered that he was outside again while the congregation inside continued to sing the first hymn. The bishop stood up, brushed himself down and made his way to the main door and processed in again although I assume, having reached the sanctuary a second time, he avoided the chair in question. According to the story, the service continued without a hitch. It is, of course, not only bishops but all of us who are prone to find ourselves sometimes in an environment – by accident or design – away from God. As I have said before, there may be any number of reasons for this. We may have lost our balance in our relationships for a while, become too self-important or just given up on our faith. Whatever the reason, regardless of what has gone on and whether it is our fault or not, our praying – wherever and however we do this – will be helped if at regular intervals we take ourselves back into the presence of God with open-hearted love to receive the blessing and guidance of his Spirit. There are those who become focused on their understanding of sin in terms of what they have done or not done almost to the exclusion of their understanding of the importance of the place from which they pray which, as I suggest, should come first.

We need first of all to find the best way to spend time to be with God regularly, to be enfolded in the often unspoken prayer of his loving embrace, before we attempt to do anything with our praying. It is easy to forget that it is God who gives life and God who inspires our prayers. Just as two lovers need to spend quality time together to nurture the love they have for one another, so we need to sit in silence and cherish the gift of God's love and prayer so that we, too, may stay together.

Grounding

Going to church on a Sunday or during the week is a special means by which we go out of our way to put ourselves in the presence of God. While we are never far from the presence of God wherever we are, we might also have a corner or some place or chair at home where we go to be with God in prayer. It can be helpful at times to make a special journey – be it to church or into another room at home – by which we enter into the presence of God symbolized maybe by a lighted candle, open Bible or religious painting. Once there, we can read again the words from Genesis at the beginning of this chapter, asking ourselves how much we treat our lives – and the lives of others – as gift rather than in some other way. Our thoughts and observations that arise from this can become the focus of our prayers that follow.

Having done this, we might want to spend some time thinking about those whose lives are important to us, those closest to us whom we love. As we give thanks for all that they mean to us, we can also reflect on their lives and love as precious gifts which maybe from time to time we take for granted. We can then make another special journey to our loved ones and find a way to thank them for all they give to us, and express our desire to cherish the gift of their love for us.

Reflecting

God is love, and those who abide in love abide in God, and God
abides in them.   (1 John 4.16b)

Praying

Dear God of redeeming love
as I replace my selfish ambitions
within the garden of your love
may I learn to cherish
the gift of my life and the lives of others
that we may be with you,
held,
healed,
and made whole by you
all the days of our lives.
Amen.

4

Prayer and sacrifice

I appeal to you therefore, brothers and sisters, by the mercies of God, to present your bodies as a living sacrifice, holy and acceptable to God, which is your spiritual worship.   (Romans 12.1)

Marking time

Recently I spent some time in retreat in a convent in Oxfordshire. On arrival, I was greeted by one of the Sisters of the community who gave me a cup of tea and made me feel very welcome. She showed me to my room and gave me a tour of that part of the convent that is open to visitors. This included the chapel. I was immediately struck by the beauty of the building with its oak pews facing each other in collegiate style down the nave. Such an arrangement facilitates the saying of psalms and prayers where verses are recited alternately by those sitting on either side of the nave. It also reminds the Sisters of the presence of Christ among them at all times.

As we looked down the chapel and along the rows of pews, I noticed how directly in front of the nuns' seats, the oak floor had been worn down over the years as result of the Sisters kneeling on the bare floor. No single nun will have been responsible for the wear and tear of the floorboards in front of her but, on taking up their places, each successive generation of Sisters will have fitted into this place of prayer. Successive generations have continued the offering of faithful prayer of the community both physically – through their knees resting in the exact place where their predecessors had knelt – as well as spiritually as they have continued the tradition of prayer several times a day. Looking along the length of the stalls, I could see the wear and tear of the floorboards which undulated at equal distances along the rows, like waves in a sea of prayer. Later on that day, as I joined the Sisters at prayer, I was impressed by how the present generation faithfully and without fuss interrupts whatever they are doing in order to make their way to the chapel and kneel – in undulating lines of faith – to pray several times a day.

While prayer is central to the life of these Sisters, it would be a mistake to think that they had nothing else to do. In fact, I was amazed at how busy they were, how many different jobs they had within the community, how much had to be done to ensure that everything ran smoothly, how little time they had for themselves and how high their standards were in terms of the faithful offering of their lives to God through Jesus Christ. This, I dare say, is likely to be the case in most religious houses. We should not imagine that all those who have dedicated their lives to the religious life do nothing but rest between the times of set prayer. But what perhaps separates them more than anything else from the rest of us who try to live and pray in the wider community of the world is the nature of their dedication to the spiritual life. They have renounced the ways of the world to dedicate themselves to the way of holiness. Central to this is the way they have to make a priority of prayer so that it interrupts or even invades their daily schedules of living. It is a calling that we who try to live faithfully in busy lives all share to some degree or other.

For many of us, the greatest single obstacle to a prayer-filled life is our lack of time. We are often too busy to pray. While we would like to spend more quality time at prayer, the demands on us become too great for us to achieve this. In fact, this busyness may also be the greatest hindrance to those who are in full-time parish ministry – both lay and ordained – who struggle to achieve the prayerfulness of spirit through which God seeks to enliven his Church. It doesn't take much for society, our work, friends, church agendas and even our family commitments, or any number of other factors, to shape our way of life into one without prayer.

The need to have set times of prayer has always been a challenge for Christians. Countless books and articles have been written on this subject which show how important the life of prayer is and how difficult it is to achieve. We might assume that set times of prayer are primarily for those in religious houses and the clergy, but there are many others who faithfully choose to pursue this way of life, quietly and faithfully day by day. And just as the Sisters in the convent I visited have to work hard to fulfil their obligations in prayer so, too, do clergy and laity alike. We cannot give up on prayer simply because we find it impossible to achieve most of the time. For by trying to pray this way we are establishing two very important priorities in our spiritual life. First, we are saying that the spirit of human beings needs quality time in the company of the Spirit of God. Heartfelt communion has to be grounded in specific times of prayer despite the rush and busyness of daily life so that earth and heaven can meet within us. In most loving relationships among human beings, there need to be times of stillness in each other's presence so that at least we can keep in time with each other. And our relationship with God deserves at the very least a similar investment in quality time spent together. For when the rhythm of our lives does not keep in time with the life of God, we are likely to fall behind because he rarely calls us to stand still in our faith. Second, to make set times of prayer a priority to the extent that they are sometimes or often likely to interrupt our own schedules of housekeeping, shopping, school runs, recreation, work commitments and so on is to make a decision to orientate our lives around God. The primary way we do this is by attending church on a Sunday or during the week in community with others. But if these are the only times we remove ourselves, our bodies, from the rush of the world and present them to God, it becomes much harder to sustain our spiritual communion with him. We need times in between our church services when we can be still and find ourselves again in God.

This suggestion will irritate and frustrate many who believe this aim is simply unachievable. They will point to other ways of praying that we can use as we go about our daily lives. Conversational prayer is one way through which we can talk to God wherever we are. This is often the most common way in which people pray outside set services in church or elsewhere. Some people have their 'God-time' while swimming or walking on a treadmill in a gym. 'I had a really good time of prayer,' someone will say to us as we conjure up images of them kneeling before a cross in a cloistered setting or churchyard. As the conversation develops, we discover they were saying their prayers while ploughing their way up and down the cordoned-off slow lane in their local swimming pool. Imagine the scene at home as they pick up their swimming kit and towel. 'Just off to say my prayers,' they might call out as they close the door behind them. 'Where has Mum gone?', asks the woman's son on discovering her absence. 'Oh, she's gone to the baths to say her prayers,' replies her husband.

Personally, I have never been able to say any prayers at all while swimming for fear of drowning. It takes me all my concentration to organize my limbs to move in such a way as to keep me on the surface of the water. And the same rules apply when in the gym. I find that to stay on a treadmill at the set speed demands huge amounts of effort and concentration. I don't think I would get much further than the first line of the Lord's Prayer before shooting off the back of the runway. I can hear the reaction of the others, 'What's the matter with the vicar?', 'He's trying to say the Lord's Prayer again. You'd think he'd know better.' Others will go for a walk – sometimes with their family pet – or listen to music or do some gardening. While they are not for me, I am in no way decrying these ways of praying. In fact, I have no doubt how extremely important and effective these forms of prayer can be. But most of us also need to allow for those prayers which do not fit easily into our daily lives and cannot be said while we are doing something else we enjoy. This is the kind of prayer for which we have to make sacrifices. Even if it is only for a short while, we have sometimes to stop what we enjoy doing and learn how to be still and be prepared to put ourselves out to be with God. Otherwise there is a very real danger that our image of God – together with the prayers that are constructed around that image – are made and moulded to fit around ourselves and our chosen lifestyle. Here, as our prayers fit into the demands of daily living, it is likely that they will cease to challenge us to encounter a new way of being. To be grounded in prayer is to be grounded in a sacrificial way of life. And we are less likely to be filled with sacrificial love for others if we do not from time to time place the demands of the daily round second to our need to make ourselves exclusively present to God. This commitment to prayer is made to the exclusion of all other demands in favour of our calling to worship God. If I am to be realistic in my response to the mercies of God and make the most of my relationship with the One who is the ground of who I am, I need to understand that this – like any relationship of love – demands sacrifice.

Hallowing time

During my visit to the convent to which I referred above, I was shown a stone carving which is set aside on its own by the door of the chapel as you enter. It is a beautiful work of art displaying great sensitivity on the part of a previous Mother (leading Sister) of the community, carved in memory of one of the other Sisters. The carving shows a mother with her head tilted on one side and resting against the head of a young child she holds in her arms. It commemorates Sister Rhoda who, in a time of war, had boarded a ship in Southampton that was to take her to India where she was to work for a while. Shortly after leaving port, the ship was torpedoed in the Channel and began to sink. The passengers were helped into the lifeboats but there was insufficient room for everyone. So Sister Rhoda gave up her seat in one of the boats for a mother and her child. They survived while Sister Rhoda remained on the sinking ship and drowned.

Acts of self-sacrifice are, of course, not performed exclusively by those whose lives are grounded in Christian sacrificial prayer. The Spirit of God works in many different ways to bless humanity with divine love and to make the consequences of this love apparent, especially in times of great need. However, the fruit of faithful Christian living which is grounded in the sacrifice of prayer and worship is the contemplation and offering of sacrificial love on a day-to-day basis. Paul makes this clear by using specific words such as 'offer', 'holy', and 'well-pleasing' that were very much part of the terminology of sacrifice at the time.

Most of us are not called like Sister Rhoda to make sacrifices for others in extreme circumstances. We are much more likely to be asked to make less dramatic sacrifices in our daily lives, which nonetheless can have a significant effect on others. Our reactions on these occasions are likely to reflect the state of our faith, revealing what and who we really believe in. While our thoughts and actions are rarely devoid of self-interest, we need constant help to live a holy life, a life that bears witness to the love of God in all things. When we offer our lives sacrificially to God through prayer, an extraordinary miracle takes place. We cease to determine the significance of our actions or the events in which we are involved by whether they are good for us. We understand them in terms of whether or not they fit into the way of love, where the fulfilment of our dreams and ambitions is no longer the priority it once was. We discover another, deeper, fulfilment that comes to the human spirit concerning the well-being of others and the healing of the world.

It is rare for anyone to live this way of love without the help that comes from God. Here, the old familiar idea of who I was competes constantly with the new 'I am'. There is a sense in which we all live at the expense of others. This is particularly evident through the inequalities of the economic systems of the world. While we flourish, others die. Or we might invest in property for our long-term security and see nothing wrong in sacrificing the needs of tenants for our own good. Or we might simply take advantage of those who are willing to help and support us. To turn this around requires more than human strength and determination. It requires sacrifice.

The strength and insight we require to make sacrifices for those around us without feeling resentful ourselves, comes primarily from those times when we are still in our exclusive attention to God. The faith that can move mountains comes only by the mercies of God and that sacrificial love which is given by grace to those who willingly and regularly put themselves in the way of God to the exclusion of other demands on their time. For it is most of all in this stillness that we are filled and refilled with the grace and power of the Spirit which we need in order to lead a holy and acceptable life. Otherwise, our faith becomes full of good intentions and clever words where our love of God, rather than informing our identity, is replaced to a greater or lesser extent by our selfish love of ourselves. We sell others short on the life of prayer because we insist on inventing every excuse not to live it ourselves. We may imagine ourselves as sacred vessels into which God longs to pour his life (Acts 2.17, 18 and 33), but if we do not take time to present ourselves, empty of our ambition for power in this world, how can his love flow into us?

Grounding

If you are not doing so already, set aside a time each day, or a certain number of times a week, when you can be at prayer to the exclusion of all else. This does not necessarily have to last long. The important thing is that from time to time, our priority is to be with God.

It may well be that in our present circumstances, we are not able to do this. If this is so, it is important that we do not engage in some kind of self-condemnation. But it may be that our lives will change in the future. Then we may have greater opportunity to engage in this form of sacrificial prayer.

If you do already have regular set times of prayer, try and focus from time to time on the sacrifice of time you are making to God in relation to the sacrifice of yourself in the world. In other words, ask yourself how good you are at making the link between giving yourself to God and giving yourself in the service of others.

In addition, at this stage, you might like to consider developing or rediscovering one of the following practices in prayer:

- Saying grace at meal times.
- Kneeling to say your prayers or some of them, at least.
- Using a prayer stool which will mean that your knees are on the floor (or the ground) while your back is in a comfortable position.
- Sitting upright on a firm chair with a straight back with your hands, palms upward, resting in your lap in an attitude of self-offering.
- Lighting a candle as a specific act in prayer.
- Placing a cross or crucifix or icon in front of you to focus your attention.
- Making the sign of the cross over yourself before and after prayer. This can signify the offering of your whole self to God in prayer (at the beginning) and the offering of your life to the world (at the end).

Reflecting

Or do you not know that your body is a temple of the Holy Spirit within you, which you have from God, and that you are not your own? For you were bought with a price; therefore glorify God in your body.   (1 Corinthians 6. 19–20)

Praying

Heavenly Father,
accept the prayerful offering
of my life.
Use it
according to your holy will
for the renewal of humankind
and the redemption of the world.
Amen.

Part 2

GROWING THROUGH PRAYER

5

Prayer and passion

'I will get up and go to my father, and I will say to him, "Father, I have sinned against heaven and before you; I am no longer worthy to be called your son; treat me like one of your hired hands."'
(Luke 15.18–19)

The need to make good decisions

As we have seen, it is God who both initiates and empowers our prayers. Now, as we move from looking at ways in which we can be grounded through prayer, we are aware that it is also by the operation of the Holy Spirit that we need to grow through prayer. This may appear to suggest a rather pessimistic view of human nature. Surely it is possible to become a better person by our own strength without having constantly to rely on God. Human reason together with our observation of the consequences of helpful and unhelpful behaviour should be sufficient for us to work out a way to become better people who promote more caring societies. But while we have to take responsibility for the way we live, human goodness on its own cannot grant humanity the redemption it seeks. If we are to achieve our full potential, we need not only to be good but godly as well. In other words, if we are to live and work for the preservation of creation and the advancement of humanity, we need to adopt the characteristics of the creator without at the same time trying to take sole responsibility for everything. Having been given dominion over the earth (Genesis 1.28), it is as if we are meant to share responsibility with God for our well-being and that of the planet. By adopting God-like qualities ourselves, we are more likely to co-operate with the creator God in the fulfilment of his purposes. As the Christian becomes more involved in this godly way of life he or she becomes increasingly focused on Christ. Here, as we live with Christ, or more specifically 'in Christ', the indwelling God fills us with a love that unites us with him and flows through us to the world. A life lived 'in Christ' is the life of redemptive love. 'So if anyone is in Christ, there is a new creation: everything old has passed away; see, everything has become new!' (2 Corinthians 5.17).

At one level, this appears to be a compelling way to promote the happiness and well-being of all. Why would anyone want to do anything else? Why destroy life rather than promote it? Unfortunately, our experience of life is that the attraction to live a God-denying life is huge. It can appear to be more enjoyable and requires less effort. It's easier to ignore the welfare of others and do what the hell you like. And often we don't have to go very far to find this attitude. Even those closest to us can for some reason or other adopt a way of life that worries us in its degree of wantonness. And few of us could ever say with any confidence that we would not behave in a similar way if the circumstances of our lives changed dramatically. Human beings have a special responsibility to promote a God-ward trend in life but they can only achieve this within the context of a fallen world. While some will try and make good decisions, there will be others who prefer to make decisions that at their worst promote evil. While God created a good world, creation has an undeniable shadow to it where confusion and godlessness prevail. While Christians aim to live in the light, there are others who prefer darkness. The Christian faith is nothing if not realistic both about the heights we can achieve and the depths of inhumanity to which we can sink when the pursuit of godliness is forgotten or ignored. But the good news of Jesus Christ teaches us how we can celebrate the good desires and overcome the destructive desires of human nature as our lives are caught up in the life of Christ.

As Christians we not only seek personal fulfilment, we also hope to have a transforming effect on the world around us. But we are unable to do this without the love that dispels the shadows of our godlessness. Even those most persuaded of the need to be godly, find achieving this very difficult. And sometimes as we seek to promote godly behaviour, we end up promoting godlessness. Churches can inflict terrible pain, sometimes on their own members. It is not unusual to hear of faithful members of a congregation ostracized by the majority because something they have done has been deplored as unchristian. Sometimes we adopt devilish ways in our dealing with others and should be justifiably reproved; on many occasions we can become casualties of the righteous indignation of others. But there is a sense in which everyone has to admit to unregenerate behaviour. Most people invariably fail to live by the love of Christ all the time. So what? So long as we refuse to give up and keep trying to be godly while not condemning others, we will be 'in Christ' if only by his grace and spiritual blessing of our lives. St Paul clearly struggled with this: 'For I do not do what I want, but I do the very thing I hate' (Romans 7.15). He finds the only way to deal with this is through his union with Jesus Christ, for he encourages his readers to know, 'There is therefore now no condemnation for those who are in Christ Jesus. For the law of the Spirit of life in Christ Jesus has set you free from the law of sin and death' (Romans 8.1–2). Here the most powerful and effective way to begin to change the way we behave is by the prayerful union of our lives with God through Jesus Christ. This is the only way we can remain Christ-centred, this union being the most effective source of the strength we need to live godly lives. We pray that we may learn how to make good decisions so that we might live peaceably with ourselves and others.

As creatures of free will, we have to commit ourselves to the pursuit of prayerful love in union with the universal Christ or live in darkness and isolation. At the same time as we pursue the way of love, we become increasingly aware of the battle in which we are now engaged. As we promote love, we are likely to discover even more that hatred can overcome love, self-promotion can replace self-sacrifice, bitterness can cloud our need to forgive, and retribution rather than reconciliation can become our aim and the aim of others. In this sense, all prayer is offered at the foot of the cross where we plumb the depths of God-forsakenness while at the same time asking God to forgive our enemies. The result of this fusion of divine and human energy in prayer is the godliness that was uniquely evident in the life of Jesus but which is also the way of life for all those who would follow him.

Returning home

The predominant way in which we can fuse our energies with the divine Spirit of creation is through our prayerful union with God. In order to move away from the shadow of 'survival at the expense of others' to the 'sacrificial love which cares equally for all', we need to try as best we can to live according to – and become one with –

the energies of love that lie at the heart of creation and at the heart of God. 'In itself prayer is nothing else than a devout setting of our will in the direction of God in order to get good, and remove evil.'[7]

St Luke has provided us with the moving story told by Jesus of two sons and their loving father, from which we can learn much about how we might begin to become prayerfully passionate people. Often referred to as the parable of the Prodigal Son, the story focuses on the behaviour of a wayward son and the reaction of his father and brother. The younger son asks his father for his inheritance – due usually only after his father's death – and leaving home, squanders it on dissolute living. The other son stays at home, always works hard and makes no demands on his father. When the money runs out and he is reduced to eating the food of animals, the younger son resolves to return to his father and seek his forgiveness. The words at the beginning of this chapter are the ones he rehearses in the hope his father might forgive him sufficiently to allow him at least to work for him as a slave. As soon as the father sees his son returning home, he is so overjoyed that he runs to meet him. He welcomes him home and throws a party in his honour. Instead of joining in the celebrations willingly, the elder son – for whom his father has never organized even a small celebration to honour his hard work and loyalty – resents his father's generous and forgiving spirit.

This is a multifaceted story, but for our purposes we need to focus on where the prayer and the passion come together in the story. We saw earlier that prayer can be described as a dialogue between human spirit and divine Spirit. And the words at the beginning of the chapter, rehearsed by the wayward son and repeated in the father's presence, are a prayer that arises out of his disillusionment in the passions or affairs of the world. We come across this today perhaps most of all among those who return to their faith, having taken it for granted in the past. Like this son, we can also rehearse these words and use them in our passionate longing to return to God. Fed up with and unfulfilled by the materialism and self-indulgence of the Church and of our society, we seek to walk away from all of this and become closer to the Father. We long for the purity of his embrace that comes through our repentance. So the aim of this passionate prayer is to overcome the desires of our hearts that we might become passionately involved in the life of Christ. Here, prayerful longing facilitates the fusion of human and divine energies. By this prayerful surrender we are reunited with God while at the same time dealing a death blow to the darker side of our nature. As we come to our senses, we realize that we cannot return to the embrace of God's love until we are committed to leaving our shadows behind.

The elder son in the story did not realize how blessed he was. He was always in his father's presence but even here – or perhaps because he was never far away from his father – he had forgotten the need to deal with his own darker side. He comes across as a rather begrudging character who was also taking his father's love for granted. He lived in the presence of his father and was no longer aware of the blessings of his father's love. He represents those of us who, having become so used to our Christian faith and church membership that we think almost nothing of it, have forgotten how important it is that we never take love for granted. When our relationship with Christ consists of dutiful behaviour, we exclude ourselves from his divine embrace and begrudge others who do receive it. Whether we feel that we are far away from God or whether we are keenly aware of his presence with us, we need to deal with our passions by becoming even more passionate about God. We do this by returning regularly to him regardless of whether we feel we are living under his roof, as it were, or under the stars.

Being mindful of God

It is here, in our returning, that our praying can become most intense. It is here that we have to own up to our darker side and commit ourselves to engage in constant battle with it. For while our praying is empowered by the Spirit of God, we need to bring this power to bear on our negative instincts and passions if we are to have any chance of growing in divine love. And while our praying takes place in the depths of our spirits, in returning we have to engage the healing power of the Spirit with our minds. The younger son had a change of mind brought on by his recognition of his pitiful circumstances. Mindful of this, he understood that the language of love frequently involves saying sorry. The elder son also needed a change of mind. We can only hope that having heard his father's explanation of his behaviour in welcoming the younger son back home, he too would have said sorry.

We should be mindful of our need of repentance to allow the Spirit to confront and change the decisions we make and the way we behave. If our daily prayers involve a journey of return to the mercy of God, we need to rehearse the words of the younger son – or some similar expression of sorrow – each time we invite God's love to embrace our sometimes bruised and broken hearts. By repentance we learn about the love that welcomes and forgives in such a way that our worldly desires and passions are transformed.

Living as we do in a world that has fallen out of love with God, every time we come to prayer we should remind ourselves of our constant need to return to him. For it is likely that from time to time we will have drifted away from him or that we will have taken our faith for granted. As part of this returning, we acknowledge our neediness and rehearse the language of prayerful surrender to God in Jesus Christ. Empowered by prayer, we are given the opportunity to celebrate daily the love of God.

The word 'repentance' as used in the New Testament refers literally to having a change of mind or going through a process where the mind is constantly renewed (Romans 12.2). It can be described as a once-for-all moment which is continually repeated whenever we pray. Here, as we allow the Holy Spirit to draw us into the presence of Christ, we also invite him to get to work on our mind. It may well be that the words of the younger son – rehearsed and repeated in the story – were the formula of a confession Luke would have known from regular use in the early days of the first Christian communities. Those of us who comprise the Church today and have been given free will to accept or reject the love of God any number of times on any given day, need, therefore, to make up our minds every day to return to Christ. It may even be appropriate to repeat the words of this early confession at some stage every time we pray.

We can make this confession by reflecting on the circumstances of our lives and, more specifically, on where we are in relation to God. We may have walked away and become immersed in our own selfish delights, in which case we need to make up our minds to return to the Father as soon as possible. Or we may be feeling that our life and faith are going well enough and have not noticed that the love of our hearts has gone cold. Here, we need to move into the passionate and arduous prayer of surrendering our passions to God, admitting them first and then seeking forgiveness. We follow this by inviting the Spirit of God to envelop us in the love of God so that our godlessness is overcome by the embrace of healing grace. At this point we can name our dark desires and invite healing for each one so that by the power of God (always more powerful than demonic energies) they can be transformed. And whenever we feel we are likely to return to unhelpful behaviour in our dealing with others or ourselves, we can remind ourselves of our change of mind and commitment to live in Christ.

Making our confession has always been an important part of the prayers of the Church. According to our tradition and preference, we might say sorry to God with others in corporate prayer or through an ordained minister or soul friend. We may prefer simply to say sorry when we are saying our prayers on our own. Having done this, we ask God to draw us back again into his presence through the proclamation of his healing love or absolution. When we engage in this process – rather than just going through the motions – the effect on our spiritual awareness can amaze us. We can feel much closer to God. When we don't do this, we can be surprised at the distance we have put between ourselves and him.

Passionate prayer – like much passionate behaviour – is based on a strong yearning or longing. If we are to put ourselves in that place in relation to the Father's love where his Spirit challenges us to overcome our godlessness, we have at the same time to long for our Father's love. So the prayer of the repentant heart that enables us to struggle with our darkest thoughts and demonic behaviour comes out of our longing to be with God. And this unites us with his creative energy, the sacrificial love that itself longs to bring us home safe and sound.

Grounding

If you don't do this already – or haven't done so for a while – try to combine this 'returning to the Father' as a regular part of your life of prayer. It can at times precede or immediately follow on from your prayer of 'Here I am' which we looked at in Chapter 1. Make time so that having returned, you can engage your mind with the Spirit in prayer, asking the Spirit to fill you with his strength and love and thereby transform your darker desires. You might like to make an act of surrender to God, perhaps by kneeling or lying on the floor face down. Engage your mind with your spirit in this, and do not be surprised if you have to struggle with your own pride and passion. Having become this passionate in prayer once, go on longing, returning and struggling in thanksgiving and celebration of the God who longs to welcome us all home.

Reflecting

Or do you suppose that it is for nothing that the scripture says, 'God yearns jealously for the spirit that he has made to dwell in us'? But he gives all the more grace; therefore it says,
'God opposes the proud but gives grace to the humble.'
Submit yourselves therefore to God. Resist the devil, and he will flee from you. Draw near to God, and he will draw near to you. (James 4.5–8a)

Praying

Loving Father of the universe,
through my longing for your spirit and strength
please welcome me home.
Forgive my wayward desires
and transform my ingratitude
into a graceful acceptance
of your transforming love.
Amen.

6

Prayer and the night

—◆◆◆—

But when they saw him walking on the lake, they thought it was a ghost and cried out; for they all saw him and were terrified.

(Mark 6.49)

Watching and waiting

As a parish priest, when I am visiting someone who is going through a difficult time of their life one of the questions I tend to ask is whether they are able to sleep at night. This is because we all need to sleep so our bodies – and in particular our minds – can rest. If our ability to rest is limited in difficult times, our ability to cope with the pressures that are on us can rapidly decrease. How many hours we need to sleep can be affected by any number of factors, such as the natural rhythms of our brain functions, our age, health and so on. Some of us can cope on little sleep with any amount of stress and pressure. Most of us, I suspect, need quality rest that comes from several hours' sleep at night. When we are unable to benefit from the amount of sleep we need, we can end up feeling not only tired but short-tempered and unable to think clearly and make decisions.

Sometimes when we are worried about something, we find it difficult to go to sleep at night or, having gone to sleep, we wake up about half an hour later and are unable to get back to sleep, with our concerns very much to the forefront of our minds. When this happens, we can develop our own strategies to cope with being awake at night. We might, for example, make ourselves a hot drink, read a book, watch television, or catch up with our emails. We might also decide to use this time for prayer. When I have been in this situation and used the time to pray for others, I have discovered that concentrating on them and their needs has meant that my own concerns have not bothered me as much. Having prayed like this, I find I can go back to sleep again. This may appear to be a very selfish reason to pray for others, and nothing other than a technique to calm the brain; but while it may begin as such, with practice we can find that we start to use this time not so much for ourselves as for the good of others. It is also a special opportunity – when all is still and quiet – to be aware of the presence of God, who himself becomes the context of our prayers rather than these being dominated by our own needs and neuroses.

Prayers in or through the night – vigils and prayer watches – have for many centuries been part of the prayer of religious orders and a special offering of prayer by others at certain times of the year or when communities or nations have faced special challenges. Today vigils are kept in parish churches particularly on the evening of Maundy Thursday in Holy Week as we recall the betrayal and arrest of Jesus, or on the night of Holy Saturday as we wait to welcome the Risen Christ with the dawn of Easter Sunday. We may also attend prayer vigils at times of national crisis, or for special reasons such as to pray for the peace of the world.

Prayer through the night, therefore, can become a part of our life of prayer either because of a need of our own or as part of our inter-cessory prayer for others and for the world. We may also use this as a time when we can concentrate on our own awareness of God and our individual growth in faith. Together with our prayers during the day, it leads us to an even greater union with God as we seek in-creasingly that freedom of spirit that comes when we live within the harmonies of creation, 'when I think of you on my bed, and meditate on you in the watches of the night; for you have been my help, and in the shadow of your wings I sing for joy. My soul clings to you; your right hand upholds me' (Psalm 63.6–7).

Taking heart in prayer

When praying through the night comes as a result of some unwanted pressure in our lives, we can feel as if we are straining at the oars of a boat against an adverse wind. This was the situation the disciples found themselves in when, having struggled through the night, in the early light of the dawn (literally, in the fourth watch of the night) they mistook Jesus for a ghost. As Mark records the story, Jesus had been alone and at prayer on a mountain, having told the disciples to go ahead, cross the lake and meet him at Bethsaida on the other side. Jesus comes to them walking on the water, so it is small wonder that they are frightened by his appearance. But Mark is saying that at a time when they were on their own and facing difficulties, the disciples should have recognized Jesus. He goes on to tell us that the cause of their lack of understanding was that their hearts were hardened. They were so impervious to the message of Jesus at this stage in their discipleship, they had not understood the meaning behind the feeding of the five thousand: that Jesus was the Messiah. As Mark puts it, 'they did not understand about the loaves' (6.52). When Jesus sees their fear and misunderstanding, his first words are, 'Take heart, it is I; do not be afraid' (Mark 6.50). It appears, therefore, that the ability to recognize Jesus as the one through whom God was changing the world of human relationships depended upon the condition of the disciples' hearts. We may interpret the heart here as a reference to the core of ourselves, the very centre from which we live and where our prayers are grounded. So, for prayer through the night to be effective in helping us to accept the love of Christ, rather than seeing only the ghosts of unexpected and unwelcome fears that haunt us, we need especially at this time to open our hearts to him.

We engage in praying through the night not only when we cannot sleep but also when we have made a conscious decision beforehand to spend this time in prayer for others we know, or for the needs of the world, or because life is problematic for us. Here, sometimes, we can adopt a combative stance with God. We may feel resentful that life has turned out as it has. We might call out and demand to know why someone we know and love is suffering through ill health, or why innocent children suffer through warfare, famine and natural disaster in the way they do, or why we have to go through hellish experiences we could well do without. Tired from struggling to make sense of life, we blame God for the woes of the world. The disciples might well have felt like this as they struggled to get across the lake. While they did not fully understand Jesus at the time, they were following him at least because they thought he was God's appointed messenger who was going to help the people of Israel win in their struggle over the forces of Roman occupation. It was Jesus' fault, therefore, that they were in the boat at night when certainly some of them – probably those who were fishermen – knew it was not a good time to be out as far as the weather was concerned. Mark goes on to tell us that having told the disciples not to be afraid, Jesus gets into the boat and the wind dies down.

Some may understand this calming of the wind to mean that Jesus has the power to overrule the forces of nature when they are against us. Or we might interpret it to mean that when we invite him to be with us, Jesus can rescue us from those things that threaten to annihilate us, not least our anger at God. And even in the most frightening or life-threatening circumstances, we can pray with peaceful purpose when we invite Christ to be with us. It may be that we are meant to remind ourselves that while we may blame God for the problems we face, he is not against us – in the sense that he is causing us to suffer – but is on our side. So, when we are at prayer in difficult times, during the night – literal and metaphorical, if we can look beyond ourselves in an open-hearted way, we may well make out the presence of Christ as he reveals God to us in all that we are going through. Catching sight of the glory of God through Jesus at times such as these can bring us great comfort in the darkness of the night or the dawn of a new day.

There do, however, seem to be occasions when we are allowed to go through difficult times so that we might grow in faith. In telling the disciples to sail on their own at night across the lake, Jesus may well have been testing their faith in him. There can be little doubt that their faith and knowledge of him will have grown significantly by the time they reached Bethsaida. In this sense, the problems the disciples were experiencing were not the result of God working *against* them but purposefully *with* them through difficult times. In similar circumstances we may also want from time to time to express our frustration and anger in prayer, blaming God for making life so difficult and not intervening when it makes most sense to do so. But if we persist in this, we are likely not only to deny his presence in our prayers but also the compassionate love which he offers to bring us through this test.

In company with these disciples, we may find that because we might not understand the full meaning of the life and teaching of Jesus, there will always be times when it becomes a great strain to move our lives on to that place where we feel strongly that God is calling us to be. Many laity and clergy who have struggled with their vocation to serve God will be familiar with this. We can have an overriding sense that God is calling us to 'cross to the other side of the lake' to a new way of life or a new ministry or new relationships but, despite many prayers, the way ahead remains unclear. Instead of being able to see clearly in daylight, we remain frightened by the darkness of the night. We cannot yet work out how best to react to our sense of vocation, and every time we try and respond faithfully and prayerfully, the way ahead is still in doubt. We are left feeling that 'someone or something' is getting in the way. It's as if there is a force actively working against us, to frustrate God's purpose for our lives.

There may be a physical reason why we cannot move on as we want. Or it may be that there are forces beyond our control that are making any kind of progress in prayer really difficult. We may feel that we are struggling against the emotional disarray and psychological imbalance of others or our own inability to overcome the powers and passions that can dominate us. These and many other 'demons' prowl around our bedrooms and cause us spiritual and emotional disarray. But we can become so focused on our problems and messed up by them that we forget that we are engaged in a spiritual battle which often manifests itself through a life-threatening darkness of the mind and spirit. At times such as these, we need to remind ourselves to pray for protection. The late-night service of Compline which we may say last thing before we go to bed includes this power-ful prayer that we can use when we cannot go to sleep, or when we wake in the night: 'Visit, we beseech thee, O Lord, this place, and drive from it all the snares of the enemy; let thy holy angels dwell herein to preserve us in peace; and may thy blessing be upon us evermore; through Jesus Christ our Lord. Amen.'[8] This is a prayer that has brought protection to many generations of Christians over the years.

Looking out for Jesus

One of the reasons why the disciples failed to recognize Jesus as the Messiah may have been because they had inherited very fixed ideas about where the Messiah was to be found and how he would behave. For example, most of them certainly didn't appear to think he was to be crucified. In a similar fashion, when praying through the night we need not only to look out for Jesus in order to catch a glimpse of the glory of God as it engages predictably with the suffering of the world, but we also need to be sufficiently open-hearted to be able to recognize him where we least expect to see him.

I can remember one occasion not so long ago when I was moving house, taking some household rubbish in the back of my car to the local refuse collection centre. Instead of reversing as usual, for some reason I parked my car head-on to the container I was going to use the most. I did so with some trepidation as on a previous trip, a gentle giant of a young man in his twenties had pointed out to me that I was putting some of my recyclable rubbish in the non-recyclable rubbish containers. So my heart was in my mouth as I waited for the big man to emerge from the shadows. He knew me by now. He was a lovely man, approachable and kind but I couldn't cope with another bag-ripping, possessions-spilling, heart-wrenching episode. As I peered warily through the windscreen, I noticed something as extraordinary as it was unexpected. Jammed into the handle of the refuse container in front of me was a beautiful wooden crucifix. I would expect to see a crucifix in a church or on a memorial or hung around a person's neck. I would never have thought of seeing one hanging haphazardly like this in a council rubbish tip.

'Lofty' was on his way over. It was going dark again. 'Dear Lord, spare me from another public flogging,' I thought. As his shadow approached, I got out of the car and, pointing to the crucifix, asked him if he knew why it had been placed on the side of a rubbish container. He wasn't sure. It wasn't something he or his workmates had done. After a short discussion, we came to the conclusion that someone hadn't been able to bring themselves to throw it away with the rest of their possessions. How on earth do you work out which container you are going to consign Jesus to? (Personally, I think he recycles pretty effectively – from one generation to another – but others might disagree.) Whoever had left the crucifix behind had perhaps placed it somewhere where someone else would see it and take responsibility for it. As the big man and his colleagues had no use for it, I asked him if I might take it and keep it safe. He said he was very happy for me to do so. So I took the crucifix home and kept it on my desk. Being roughed up on a rubbish heap hadn't actually done any damage to it. It was in excellent condition.

Some months later, speaking at a conference about church growth for local clergy, I told this story about the crucifix that now sits on my desk. At a time when many churches find it difficult to make contact with their local communities, I thought it significant that I had come across this figure of the crucified Christ in a refuse collection centre. Cast out once again from people's lives, he had been consigned to the rubbish tip.

Following my talk, a local vicar attending the conference came up to me and took me to one side. He asked me to describe the big man to him. As I did so a look of recognition came over his face. The rubbish tip was in his parish and he had recently taken 'Lofty's' funeral. Apparently, soon after passing his driving test and on his way to work, he had misjudged his speed as he approached a round-about, with tragic consequences. Both my colleague and I were left speechless at this point as my story – I had told no one about it before – and the tragic death of his parishioner came together. We were suddenly aware of perhaps another reason why this crucifix had ended up on the rubbish heap and why the attention of the big man had been drawn to it by a priest. I also wondered whether I had been right to remove it. It's almost as if there are times in our lives when we are unwittingly used to give others the opportunity to draw closer to God through very unlikely circumstances and, not least, by our prayers. It's as if there are special times when God wants to assure us of his love, especially when we experience shadows that frighten and even threaten our very existence. It's as if there are messages left for us and our loved ones that there is more to life than meets the eye. At the foot of the cross, fear is met by faith and we should therefore always watch out for Christ, especially in the most unlikely or difficult times of prayer.

When approaching the boat and seeing how terrified the disciples are, Jesus says, 'Take heart, it is I; do not be afraid' (Mark 6.50). The words 'it is I' translated literally are 'I am'. This formula for the divine identity of Jesus, to which we have already referred, is not given to us by Mark with the same emphasis of meaning that John gives it in the Fourth Gospel. From the beginning, John proclaims Jesus as the pre-existent Word of God. There is no mistaking the divinity of Christ who says, 'The Father and I are one' (John 10.30). But Mark takes a different approach. He often hides or obscures the messiah-ship of Jesus, preferring to call him the Son of Man. So when we come across these words, hidden as it were in the text, we become even more aware of the significance of this saying. Used here in the way it is by Jesus, it is as if Mark is referring us to the hidden 'I am' within all of us. Maybe, it is especially in the night-time of prayer that we need to be most aware that the hidden Christ who lives in us all can be recognized in heartfelt hope. Maybe we have to learn that the answer to our prayers is not found, after all, in persuading

God to save us. Perhaps, as we pray for help we need to understand that we hold the answers to our prayers ourselves. If 'I am' to make sense of God's vocation for my life then 'I am' responsible for making decisions that will save myself and others in order that we might do God's will. Maybe the nature of my prayers to God in heaven, in this case, has obscured the Christ who comes to me in the midst of – rather than apart from – the mess I am in.

Grounding

A prayer to use if we are awake at night or in the early morning and have decided to use this time of peace and quiet to grow closer to God:

> Lord Jesus, it was at night that you taught Nicodemus the mystery of our rebirth in water and the Spirit. As we keep vigil this night to hear your Word, bring to birth in us the new self which is your own creation, and we will come to the light and live by the truth, today and for ever.[9]

Or you might like to use either or both of these prayers if you are awake at night and have decided to use this time of peace and quiet to pray for others:

> Lord our God, as we keep watch this night we commend all people and their lives to you. We remember in particular all those who are working, those who in their suffering cannot sleep, those who use the night to do evil, those who are afraid of the day about to dawn. May they all come out into the light of your Day. We ask you this through Jesus, our Lord. Amen.[10]

> Keep watch, dear Lord, with those who wake, or watch, or weep this night, and give your angels charge over those who sleep. Tend the sick, give rest to the weary, sustain the dying, calm the suffering, and pity the distressed; all for your love's sake, O Christ our Redeemer. Amen.[11]

Reflecting

I bless the LORD who gives me counsel;
in the night also my heart instructs me.

I keep the LORD always before me;
because he is at my right hand, I shall not be moved.

(Psalm 16.7–8)

Praying

Jesus,
in the darkness of the night
I take heart
in you
as you take heart in me.
Amen.

7

Prayer and faith

'But your little ones, who you said would become booty, I will bring in, and they shall know the land that you have despised. But as for you, your dead bodies shall fall in this wilderness. And your children shall be shepherds in the wilderness for forty years, and shall suffer for your faithlessness, until the last of your dead bodies lies in the wilderness.' (Numbers 14.31–33)

Holding on

For years, whenever I cooked a meal at home the description of what was about to appear on the table was always given the same prefix by my children. The answer to the question, 'What's for tea?' should have been something like 'fish fingers and chips' or 'beans on toast' but they would invariably add the prefix 'Burnt'. The forbearance of my children while crunching their way through various forms of charcoal was admirable, as was their sense of humour. I eventually decided that I would have to cease delivering up burnt offerings which appeased nobody. So, with the help and advice of others, I taught myself to cook half decently so that tea nowadays consists mostly of fresh food that has been cooked reasonably well.

To achieve this I realized early on that I would have to follow the cooking instructions very carefully. But I also discovered that when things went wrong, I could still end up with the result I wanted even if I had to achieve it by a roundabout method. While most of us can follow a recipe, a great sense of achievement in cooking can come when we end up with the result we wanted, having at some stage found ourselves in a position where all seemed lost.

There are many other ways in our daily living where we can take the long way round to get to where we want to be, so long as we keep faith in ourselves and what we are trying to do. Sometimes, when we are trying to explain something to someone else, we can feel we have eventually 'got there' although we may have used many more words or explanations than were strictly required in order to pass on the information. Or we may find that we have become lost while walking in the countryside. By keeping a calm head and working out from the map where we have ended up, we can still find our way home. On one occasion, I can remember making an unexpected detour in the Lakeland Fells due to inclement winter weather. I came down the opposite side of a ridge from the one I had planned. My priority had been to get my shivering spaniel companion off the hill before he froze to death. In an unfamiliar and deserted valley I consulted my map and eventually worked out where we were and calculated the extra seven miles I would have to walk while George, the dog, peered over my shoulder from his position in my rucksack.

I have lost count of the times when I have been trying to live a God-centred and prayerful life only to find myself in a place where I have felt as if I am miles from his presence and intended purpose for my life. In so many ways and on so many occasions, we can discover that to pray with faith is not so much about travelling in a straight line from A to B as it is about clinging on for dear life because we've got lost again.

A patient attitude to every ordeal makes the regenerated soul more able to apprehend the 'wisdom from above' (James 3.17). In some hidden place within her she finds 'a well of water springing up into everlasting life' (John 4.14). Prayer is like a strong hand clinging fast to God's raiment, at all times and in all places: in the turmoil of the crowd, in the pleasant hours of leisure, in periods of loneliness.[12]

When God takes us the long way round

There was a story told some fourteen hundred years before the birth of Jesus Christ about how the Israelites refused to hold on to their faith even when so many of their prayers had already been answered in very special – if not spectacular – ways.

This was a time when the Hebrew slaves had been led by Moses out of imprisonment and impoverishment under the Pharaoh in Egypt into the wilderness of the Sinai Peninsula. Along the way they had been miraculously delivered from the pursuing Egyptian charioteers who drowned in the waters of the Red Sea through which the Hebrew people had escaped. All along the way, they had been aware that God had been responsible for their deliverance. It was he who was guiding them along a route where there was food and water as they made their way to a land which he had promised they would eventually inhabit for themselves.

You would think they would be enormously grateful along every step of the way. Their lives had been completely changed by the intervention of a faith – mediated by Moses – that meant they could make a fresh start. They had rediscovered their faith not only in God but also in themselves. At the stage at which the episode referred to above took place, they were going through a period of transition – they were two years into their journey through a wilderness en route to their final destination – and the future promised to be very good. Through the faith God had shown in them, together with their faithful response, they were now free from all that had previously enslaved them. They were about to inherit their own land which, far from being a desert, was full of sources of good food.

Then it all went wrong. Rather than persevering in their prayerful dialogue with God, the Hebrew people allowed their fears to defeat their faith: so much so that they said they would rather return to Egypt and become slaves again than risk all in the pursuit of what had been their divinely inspired dream. They changed their minds when they heard a report from those sent out to spy out the land they were later to claim as their own. The spies had had a close look at the Promised Land and had noted that there were already people living in this area who would fight hard to keep the Hebrew people out. I suppose the reaction of the Israelites is understandable. They decided it was preferable to be an alive slave than a dead member of an invasion force – and who could blame them? Well, according to the story, God blamed them. In fact, he was so exasperated by their lack of faith that he decided none of the adult generation would survive – with one or two exceptions – to see the Hebrew people enter the land God had promised: instead of taking a little over two years to make the journey from Egypt to Israel, God made sure it took them 40 years. So, following their falling-out with God, the Hebrew people wandered off back into the desert, and some 37 years later returned to the same place, as they prepared a second time to head off for the Promised Land.

Whatever actually happened, it is a story from which we can learn much about the way we pray and the way God answers our prayers. Like the Hebrew people we can find ourselves – through impatience or a fear of what may lie ahead – refusing to hold on to our faith in prayer. The presence and guiding hand of God may have been very real in the past. We may feel we owe God a great deal for the way in which we have been freed from situations, emotions or people that held us back and tied us down. But despite this, and maybe because of the threatening behaviour of others or the threat of allowing our faith to bring about a radical change in us, we can end up preferring the familiarity of our former lives to the greater possibilities to which God is beckoning us. Here God sometimes takes us the long way round because of our lack of faith in him when we contemplate the challenges that lie ahead.

It is natural not to want to risk everything but, in terms of the kingdom about which Jesus spoke so much, how much we are prepared to give can determine how much we receive. The God who wants to give us an abundant spiritual life cannot fill us with his life if we are not prepared to empty ourselves of our old ways. The journey to the place where our lives are likely to make most sense does not always follow a straight line between two points. Invariably we are taken a longer way round. And when this happens and we feel our prayers are getting us nowhere, we can give up on them. We don't realize that there is a very good reason why the answers to our prayers are taking so long, or why God hasn't immediately taken the lives we have offered and immediately made us into saints. We might initially feel that we are standing still in our prayers but there is no such thing for those who are inspired by the Spirit of Christ, for 'those who have the mind of the Holy Spirit, sail on, even when they are asleep'.[13]

As we have seen, it is a continuous struggle to follow this way of faith. Jesus warned his disciples, 'For the gate is narrow and the road is hard that leads to life, and there are few who find it' (Matthew 7.14). In our journey of prayer, we may not feel particularly courageous most of the time, even when we know deep down that the presence of God has been very real for us. We have to cling on to our faith and also hold tight to our faith in prayer, in common with everyone else who has tried to live this way. There will always be times when we doubt that God's ways are the best, and it is then that God takes us the long way round. The result of this is that when we finally reach that place we have recognized as his destination for our lives, we are able to make the most of it and enjoy it to the full. This may be a new place to live, a new church to join, a new job, a new relationship. It may also be a new way of serving Christ, or it may even refer to that final rest, peace and joy we have been promised when we make the final journey from this life to the next. Spiritual maturity – especially in terms of our growing in and through prayer – often comes to those whose spirit grows through faithful forbearance of the circumstances God has given them. Rarely, if ever, is this particular path straightforward and undemanding. So we have to learn how important it is for us not only to hold on to our faith but also to cling on to our faithful praying if the Spirit is going to make sense of our lives.

We have already seen how important it is to make a sacrifice in terms of our dedication to times of prayer, but it is also important that we continue to pray even though we feel our hopes and dreams and the promises of God are out of reach. Someone once came to me who had a desire to grow in the Christian faith. He had been unemployed for a while and was hoping that God would lead him back to the life he once had and which he had worked hard to achieve. Yet in discussion it was apparent that the way he had been living his life previously – while there had been glimpses of God in action – had not been one through which God was willing to lead him to fulfil his vocation. He came to realize that it was no longer any good to retrace his steps in order to find the life he wanted. He had to go forwards but by a different route. He had to pursue a new way of life in order to find fulfilment. So he began to apply for a completely different kind of work from the one that he had been previously engaged in. As soon as he did this, he discovered a new vocation – quite different from his previous one – that drew him into an appreciation and understanding of himself and of God's will for his life that deep down he had always been looking for. It is unlikely he would have discovered this if he had not been taken the long way round, through a period of unemployment in which he was given the time – as he wandered about in his own wilderness – to reflect increasingly prayerfully on where God was leading him and where his future lay.

So the faithful prayer of the long way round involves a lot of holding on in hope even when it feels safer to let go and give up.

And faithful prayer also involves following a new way that excites us although we would not necessarily have chosen it for ourselves. Here the way ahead involves making difficult decisions that may even threaten the basis of our lives, so that we might become the people God has called us to be and strive for his kingdom of love in places where love is threatened.

When we go the long way round

On some occasions it feels as if God is taking us the long way round either so that we may learn to be more faithful or to grow further in faith and love. But there is another kind of situation we can encounter where we find ourselves taking the long way round because we – rather than any other influence – have made some decisions that have had the result of putting us where we shouldn't be. Faithful praying will draw us closer to God and the fulfilment of our lives. But when our praying succumbs to worldly interests we can end up in a place where we sense that our prayers no longer relate to our lives as they have done in the past. This can be the result of an over-anxious approach to fulfiling God's purpose for our lives. Or it may come from our desire to have a conventional faith when God is calling us to experiment with new ideas. Jesus once said that we cannot serve both God's and man's agendas because it is so easy to get the two confused (Luke 16.13). At times like this, faithful prayer involves our continued commitment so that we might find our way again. It also involves especially a willingness to listen to what others who are prayerful themselves have to say to us. When we have lost our way in prayer, the words of God which we hear through the prayerful presence of others can confirm that – while we think we may have made a mess of things – we are nevertheless in the right place after all.

We can take great comfort from the way this has happened even to the greatest figures in the history of the Christian story. While sometimes we like to understand their faith in terms of a perfect reaction to the presence of God, we learn much more about their prayers and ours if we allow their lack of perfection – their humanity – to speak for itself. It is often in unlikely and untidy gatherings of human beings rather than through the Church and its great institutions that God is borne to the world. God invariably surprises us when in his self-revelation, he suddenly makes sense of us.

While we assume it to be the case in our Christmas celebrations, it is unlikely that Mary and Joseph travelled to Bethlehem because they had been guided by God to fulfil what a prophet had predicted many hundreds of years previously concerning the location of the birth of their baby (Micah 5.2). They were on the road because the Romans who occupied their land had ordered everyone to return to their ancestral homes to be registered for taxation. Given Mary's advanced state of pregnancy, we may assume that she and Joseph would not have embarked on the journey from Nazareth to Bethlehem – some 70 miles – unless they really had to. At a time when childbirth was hazardous this trek, which would have taken several days, was likely to reduce the chances of a safe delivery of their unborn baby.

Joseph and Mary could have chosen to defy the law and stay at home. Many would say they should have played it safe so that the promises of God would come true in the birth of their baby. They chose instead to risk the safe delivery of their baby by obeying the law and thereby avoiding the wrath of the Roman authorities. It was a choice between obeying God or man. They chose the latter. They took a risk. They were ordinary people of extraordinary faith who were living by a unique promise of God about their future, yet even they struggled to cope with the dangers this would involve if they had decided to play it safe. When they eventually arrived in Bethlehem and Mary went into labour, on discovering that the only place in which they could stay was a stable, they must have felt they had blown it. There was no miraculous provision for them. No angelic salutation. It must have appeared as if everything was going disastrously wrong.

Mary gave birth to Jesus when she and Joseph were on their own, separated from their friends and their comfortable home in Nazareth. Despite the absence of angelic hosts, Mary and Joseph would have rejoiced at the birth of her firstborn son. But they may also have wondered whether God was still with them and whether their child really was the one promised by him to be the Saviour of the world. As a result of their recklessness, had God changed his mind about the identity of their baby? Or as a result of their desire to keep in favour with the authorities, had they somehow messed up the arrangement?

Their questions were answered with the arrival of the shepherds who came as a result of their own prayerful encounter. As they listened, these unlikely characters described to Mary and Joseph how angels had appeared to them and sent them to see the one born to be the Saviour, Messiah and Lord. While Mary and Joseph had indeed taken the long way round, they had the assurance now – through the prayers of others – that the very special divine purpose for their lives at that moment in time had been fulfilled. In fact, it may well have been because of their waywardness that this purpose was fulfilled. Unsurprisingly, we are told that Mary treasured all these words and took them to heart. While at first nothing seemed to have gone to plan on that first Christmas night, it was through the combination of great faith and doubt, conflicting loyalties to God and state, and in particular through the meeting of unlikely strangers, that the identity of Christ was revealed. Sometimes we need to hold on to promises we feel God has made us through prayer until they are confirmed by the prayerfulness of others. We may feel that we have failed to live up to his expectations. We have not lived as we have prayed. But the faithfulness of God is always far greater than our prayerful confusion.

Sometimes we domesticate our prayers by limiting God to fixed images or ideas. We invent a stay-at-home God to comply with our desire for comfort and security. At the same time we can become ensnared by institutionalized economic injustice, or caught out by the greed that takes more than is needed. Yet, especially when we are trying to do what is right and end up doing what is wrong, or when we are aiming to live a godly life and get caught up in the life of the world, the love of God brings into our lives the people of prayer whom we need to help us save ourselves. But we have to be alert and ready to listen so that our prayers may be informed by the divine dialogue in the lives of others.

When we are at our most naked and vulnerable, we can see in the nativity of Christ that we need look no further than at the generosity of love that lies at the heart of creation. Here we are introduced to those who, through their own prayerfulness, bring angelic messages of hope. They encourage us to look deeper into the mystery of God's prayers for us. For by this re-enchantment of life, we find that in dark and lonely places – on hills at night, or in our begrudging submission to those who want to burden us with their taxes and laws – we can see angels and hear the chorus of praise that is the prayerful union of heaven and earth. Here we are encouraged to pray in hope rather than to stay within the comfort zone of unalter-able relationships, fixed assets and the desire to control God.

Grounding

Take time to consider whether there are areas of your life where you need simply to hold on to God in prayer? If so, do you have a sense that God is taking you the long way round?

Take time to reflect on whether your prayers will make more sense if you link them more closely to patient attention to what others are saying to you. Is there anything that someone has said recently that has been a prayerful response to your situation or that of someone you know?

Put some time aside to reflect more deeply on the way God has led you through your life. Do you feel you are as open to God in prayer today as you should be, even in the face of an uncertain future?

Reflecting

She had heard about Jesus, and came up behind him in the crowd and touched his cloak, for she said, 'If I but touch his clothes, I will be made well.'   (Mark 5.27–28)

Praying

Jesus, I am afraid
for the way is hard
and you seem far away.
Are you cross with me or
do you want me to learn
that the longer it takes
the more prayers
I must say?

8

Prayer and doubt

————◆◆◆————

He himself is before all things, and in him all things hold together.
(Colossians 1.17)

Divine possibilities

Feelings of doubt can be deeply corrosive in a relationship of love. Even when there is no evidence to support our mental and emotional wondering, doubt can arise from amid our own insecurities and cast questions over the nature of love we have for another and the other person's love for us. Asking whether we can trust someone to whom we long to commit ourselves will take us straight to the heart of any relationship, because love and faith go together. Usually it is helpful to listen carefully to our doubts as, unaddressed, they lead to irrational behaviour on our part or leave unresolved issues that have a negative effect on our relationships. When we reflect on our doubts we reassess our beliefs and behaviour usually in relationship with others. Handled carefully, rather than being destructive, they can provide us with moments when we mature in what or whom we believe.

In the Christian life, feelings of doubt may simply creep up on us and catch us unawares, or they may arise because we are going through a period in our lives when love isn't providing us with the security and purpose to which we've become accustomed. Suddenly, our faith in God is challenged by the cooling of love that comes with doubt. Although we are aware that we are living in the presence of God, we may wonder whether what we believe takes us any closer to the truth about love and meaning, life and death. Even those who have worked out their Christian faith over many years, grounding it in prayerful devotion, can suddenly discover that their faith and love – secure and solid for so long – have slipped through their fingers as it were, even while they were praying. At times like this, we can end up wondering whether ours is a God who listens to us, or even whether he exists at all. Just as we might feel guilty about doubting the love someone else may have for us, we can also descend into a dark and lonely pit of self-doubt and guilt. Here we have to admit to ourselves that our relationship with God is not what it used to be.

We can prevent our love for someone else from growing by putting them on a pedestal, thereby removing them from the normal round of regular reappraisal that comes to those who by their co-existence have continually to change and develop. Similarly, our doubts in prayer can come about because we have made too much of a god of our beliefs to the extent that our loving has become routine and mundane. We have quenched the spring that brings us life (John 4.14) by our unshakeable conventions and convictions.

> When you turn your natural longings for the divine into a prison, then everything in you will continue to ache. The prison subverts your longing and makes it toxic. Watched by a negative God, you learn to watch your self with the same harshness.[14]

There is no need to feel guilty about having such doubts about faith and love. They have always been part of the Christian life even for those who have been most committed and regarded as most prayerful. Rarely is the path of love and faith entirely predictable. Our praying in terms of our dialogue with the divine source of that love and faith will necessarily have to adapt and develop in response to our changing circumstances and personal development.

Love is rarely simple or straightforward. Unsurprisingly, our love and faith in God are also rarely simple or straightforward. For faith is where our hopes and fears combine at the entrance to the empty tomb. It is not an environment that is immediately convincing or makes sense, in the way we usually make sense of things. But it is where truth can be found. Those who pretend that faith is uncomplicated deny those who suffer – often through no fault of their own – the deep compassion of the divine embrace that alone redeems humanity from darkness.

For those of us unsatisfied by 'easy answers fundamentalist religion' who are prepared to grapple with the meaning of love and prayer through faith – for ourselves and the good of this generation – can be led by the Spirit of Christ beyond ourselves and our sometimes limited and limiting descriptions of prayer. When we ignore the textbook approach to our spiritual development, we begin to plumb the depths of the mystery of life and love that lies at the centre of the universe. Here, by prayerful union with the Spirit of God in all things, we hold on to the truth as a treasure beyond price (Matthew 13.44) within the human heart.

So if our love or faith – and thereby our worship and praying – have been overcome by our doubting, it may well be a sign that we need to think again about these things. Instead of doubt leading to betrayal and endings, we may be surprised to find ourselves at a place where our faith and love can develop in new directions and our praying be renewed.

Casual prayer

When we regard prayer either as a mechanism to appease an angry God or as a contractual obligation to try and get the best deal for daily life, our consumerism is likely to prevent us from achieving union of body and spirit with the body and Spirit of Christ. Consumerist-type praying does nothing to develop our life with God or our love and prayers for others. Over the years, I have become convinced that while we should never give up on the practice of prayer – grounded as it is in the divine dialogue which takes place at the centre of ourselves as we become increasingly focused on the heart of the universe – we cannot engage in it if we are not open to being changed by the Spirit of life. We may have to move away from unhelpful images and models of prayer, and our hearts may have to break from time to time so that our life with God can develop.

When we divorce our praying from our being and becoming we can externalize God to the extent that our faith and love are defined by our demands. We depend on God being at our disposal. Our conversation with God resembles indistinct instructions which we shout from a train window to someone standing on the platform. The train begins to move and we continue to try and make ourselves understood above the noise of the engine and the others in the carriage with us. Meanwhile, on the platform, the one who is eager to hear what we have to say runs to try and catch us up. Inevitably the train passes the end of the platform and we lose sight of the other. We settle down without realizing the frustration we have caused for the other, and content ourselves with the thought that we can always text the remainder of our conversation later. It won't be a face-to-face conversation, but it will do. In the busyness of our lives, we treat God as if we can leave him behind. We pray casually to the God we assume cannot keep up with us rather than out of devotion to the one who is the ground of our being. We substitute text messages for a heart-to-heart conversation.

Prayer that is as casual as this, I suppose, is a bit like casual sex. Making love is the expression of the love of our hearts and minds and is supposed to be intimate, beautiful, a drawing ever closer to the other, where the needs of both are met in the deep embrace of communion. And it should be fun. When our praying is misunderstood or the casualty of thoughtlessness, our loving can become superficial, leaving our partner feeling used and further away than ever from the object of their love.

When we love someone very deeply, there are still times when sexual desires have to be met. There are occasions of frantic, physical passion where love gives way to basic needs that have to be satisfied. And similarly, in our love of God, there are times of passion when suddenly we need him for ourselves and for no other reason at all.

But if our praying is predominantly of the casual or selfish kind, we are likely to divorce or externalize our praying and loving of God from our hearts. Prayer then becomes something we do to God rather than with God.

To get away from this form of prayer abuse, we sometimes need to reassess where we believe God to be in relation to ourselves. Do we associate our praying with sacred space set aside for worship to the extent that we leave him behind when we leave these places to get on with daily life? Or do we perhaps limit our relationship with him by defining him too much in terms of being Jesus in human form? We end many of our prayers with the words, 'through Jesus Christ our Lord' because we regard Jesus as the Way to the Father (John 14.6). Yet we can end up with a concept of the presence of God that locates him in the world as a human being would be located, that is as a specific – almost human – presence in a specific location. In prayer we may think of God as standing next to us or in front of us or above us. While he may well be with us in this way, he is also 'with, in and through' us and creation at the same time. There is nowhere he is not. There is nowhere he is out of reach. He is never, as it were, standing on a railway platform as we are being borne away from him by our other commitments. Our use of sacred space in which to pray – maybe in a church or special room, or a place in our garden or a park nearby – is to do with moments when we endeavour to immerse ourselves by prayer in the loving presence of the creator. Our awareness of him may be greater in these places of prayer – maybe because others for hundreds of years have used the same place to speak and listen to God – but he is no more in these places and times than he is anywhere else.

Prayer and doubt therefore come together sometimes because we have defined God in a way that puts us at a distance – in terms of our prayerful communication – from him. Sometimes we need to think about our praying less in terms of a verbal or written communication – like a telephone conversation or text-messaging service – and more in terms of our being caught up in the energies of the love of God, the divine life of the ongoing processes of creation and re-creation. We may picture this energy in terms of springs of water or oceans of love and prayer into which we immerse ourselves as if we were swimming. Or we might imagine ourselves being enveloped by a tidal wave of love and prayer that ebbs and flows through the universe, seeking union and redemption. Either way, prayer becomes less of a contractual obligation and more of a naked embrace – an envelopment by love – where human and divine spirit unite in the ecstasy of love.

> Again it is our conviction that it is the most important task for any fully human life that we should become as open as possible to this stream of love. We have to allow this prayer to become our prayer, we have to enter into the experience of being swept out of ourselves – beyond ourselves into this wonderful prayer of Jesus – this great cosmic river of love.[15]

When prayers go unanswered

Jesus says to his followers, 'If in my name you ask me for anything, I will do it' (John 14.14). Yet sometimes – often – we pray for advice, help, support, healing, and nothing seems to happen. Nothing changes. We don't see, hear or sense the answer to our prayer. 'How can this be?', we ask ourselves. Again we turn in on ourselves. When any relationship fails, feelings of guilt and doubt are never far away. We think that maybe God doesn't answer our prayers because we have done something wrong. Perhaps we are too sinful or faithless to have our prayers answered. Again, such a reaction to failing prayer requests can come from having too anthropomorphic an idea of God.

Using the image of oceans of love we explored a moment ago helps us to understand differently issues surrounding the question of whether or not God answers our prayers. If we think about our praying in terms of our willingness to leap into a stream or even an ocean of God's love and life, to be refreshed by it, borne along by it to an unknown destination, we can reflect on the effect of our prayers quite differently. To be immersed in and also borne along by this current of love can be both exhilarating and terrifying, sometimes simultaneously so. Sometimes we need to do little ourselves to stay in midstream. At other times, we need to work hard to stay within the centre of the current. But when it feels as if we are swimming against the tide, we need only remind ourselves that if we had stayed on the bank, we would have remained uninvolved spectators, watching this river without ever having experienced its delights and depths around and within ourselves. Now, there is nothing that we do that does not affect our being and progress in this stream of love. We have become part of it. We are one with it. So wherever we are, we are surrounded by a love that bears our weight. Having taken the plunge, we find we can no longer move without its action around us or our acting upon it.

In a way, it becomes meaningless to ask whether or not a prayer has or has not been answered. It makes more sense to reflect on the way in which the nature of our very existence has been caught up in the prayer of Jesus or in the prayer of the Father through the prayer of Jesus. If we must insist on defining the response of God to our prayers in terms of their being answered or not, we can say that in this ocean of love, all prayers are answered in that they all become caught up in – or become one with – the life of the universal Christ. They are intrinsically part of him as they are of us. Everything for which we pray is already a part of this life and has eternal significance beyond our comprehension. As we pray, we perhaps alter the way in which we swim with or against the tide and also the way in which the object of our prayers is borne along towards the heart of God.

Prayer is the language of love. When two people's lives become increasingly indistinguishable, their love for one another deepens and it becomes harder to work out where one person's love stops and the other's begins. When our prayers become increasingly indistinguishable from the prayer of God that informs the core of our being, it becomes harder to work out where our prayers stop and the prayer of God begins. And the inevitable consequence of authentic love is that we rediscover ourselves within a continuous conversation within creation, and more specifically between ourselves and God, which reaches beyond the boundaries of the universe. This alters our relationship with every aspect of created matter as it, too, responds to the conversation that inspires life at all levels. In this sense, God spoke his words of creation at the beginning and they continue to this day and therefore it was – and is – very good (Genesis 1.3–31).

> My young brother asked forgiveness of the birds: it may seem absurd, but it is right nonetheless, for everything, like the ocean, flows and comes into contact with everything else: touch it in one place and it reverberates at the other end of the world . . . Everything is like an ocean, I tell you. Then you would pray to the birds, too, consumed by a universal love, as though in a sort of ecstasy, and pray that they too, should forgive your sin.[16]

Having looked, in the first two sections of this book, at how we may be grounded in prayer and how we might grow through prayer, we now proceed in the next section to consider how in this world of interrelated love, we might give to others through prayer.

Grounding

You might like to spend some time considering how doubt can inform your faith. It might be helpful to think more about how prayer incorporates you into the life of God rather than understanding it primarily in terms of a conversation between two very separate individuals.

Reflecting

> Very truly, I tell you, if you ask anything of the Father in my name, he will give it to you. Until now you have not asked for anything in my name. Ask and you will receive, so that your joy may be complete.   (John 16.23–24)

Praying

Spirit of the universe
bear my weight
in the ocean of your love
and bring me to know that I am
in touch with the world
as I am in touch with you.
Amen.

Part 3

GIVING THROUGH PRAYER

9

Prayer and compassion

———◆◆◆———

Jesus left that place and went away to the district of Tyre and Sidon. Just then a Canaanite woman from that region came out and started shouting, 'Have mercy on me, Lord, Son of David; my daughter is tormented by a demon.' But he did not answer her at all.   (Matthew 15.21–23a)

Meetings that make sense of us

In my ministry – like any other parish priest – I am no stranger to the processes of death, bereavement and grief, and there are days when experiencing these things among those you love and serve can take a heavy toll on you. On one such occasion, having spent an hour by the bedside of a parishioner who was gravely ill, my heart was lifted by something I came across a little later in a supermarket car park. Not the most obvious place, we may think, for encounters to lift the spirit. On this occasion it was the sheer simplicity and innocence of what I saw that suddenly put my feelings of sadness into a different perspective.

As I was walking to my car, I glimpsed a young mother cooing over her very young baby as she pushed him along in a shopping trolley – he was strapped into a moulded plastic seat that was too big for him and lying on his back like an astronaut in earth orbit – prior to loading him, together with the shopping, into her car.

I went over to the woman, whom I had never met before and, while I hoped she didn't think I was intruding, odd, or somehow insane, told her how grateful I was for the picture of innocence and love that she and her young son had given me. Much to my relief, she didn't treat me as if she thought I was intruding, odd, or somehow insane. In fact, we chatted for a while and it transpired that she was a cousin of a close friend of my wife. Small world, I thought.

Most of us would agree that such a coincidence is not unlikely in a town of between thirteen and fourteen thousand souls. It is more surprising, however, when we go on holiday maybe thousands of miles away from home and meet people who live just down the road from us. A friend of mine went on a trans-Atlantic cruise, only to find the person she sat next to for her first meal on board was the mother of someone whose wedding I was shortly to conduct. I am not sure whether this raised or dampened her spirits for the forth-coming voyage.

No matter how much we may sometimes want to pack up and go and live on a desert island, in the end most of us have to admit that we need to live in some kind of community with others. For to live in isolation can be to cut oneself off from those who help to provide the essentials we need for living, such as food, clothing, housing, companionship and support. The more balanced our relationships, the more human we become. I am not saying that everyone has to have a large circle of friends, just that we have to learn how best to live alongside one another because we need each other in order to survive. It is when we decide we don't need each other or a certain group of people or another nation that we begin to tear them and ourselves apart.

The Christian understanding of communion is based upon a celebration of our common humanity that finds its fullest meaning in the life, death and resurrection of Jesus Christ. By faith, love and prayer, we are called to become like Christ to the extent that he lives in us and we in him (1 John 3.24). He lives not only in us alone, of course; he lives in everyone, whether his presence is recognized or not. One of the *Common Worship* Eucharist Prayers contains the words, 'Lord of all life, help us to work together for that day when your kingdom comes and justice and mercy will be seen in all the earth.'[17] This reminds us that redemption comes as much as a result of the joint labours of different people where Christ becomes present in their love and co-operation with one another, as it does directly from God.

Some believe we meet the people we need to help us at various stages in life. There is no such thing as a coincidental meeting. When we are feeling down, we are visited by – or we come across – those who can help us. I was once on a train returning from London having watched a rugby match with my son, when I fell into chance conversation with a young man who was sitting next to me. He was returning home having attended the funeral of one of his closest friends who had died suddenly at a very early age. We talked at length about the grief and pain he was feeling and, as the conversation progressed, he asked me what I did for a living. I told him I was a parish priest and the conversation then moved on apace as he was interested to hear more about my faith. A few weeks later, I received a letter from him to say that he thought it no coincidence that we met when we did. He added that he had decided to make some major changes to his life which included becoming a Christian and leaving his job in IT to work with those in need.

In a similar way, I can recall a time when I was close to handing in my resignation in a particular parish in which I was serving because I did not feel I had the support of some of the more influential members of the congregation. I went to meet a parishioner to discuss a number of other issues related to the life of the church in question. As the meeting was nearing its end, I shared with him my frustration at what was going on. I can only describe his reply as heaven-sent. As he spoke it was as if someone else was speaking through him, giving me words of comfort and hope that changed my outlook completely.

Whether it is in car parks, high-speed trains or in our homes, it appears that we need one another for any number of reasons, not least because we need the help and support that others are meant to give us. While the word 'compassion' means literally 'to suffer with', the prayer of compassion is about how the love of God is prayerfully brought to bear on the lives of others for good. We live in a world in the process of redemption, where love triumphs at the expense of evil. Those who wish to be involved in this process through the life of Jesus Christ are called not only to be compassionate in their praying but to go further and seek out suffering – especially that which is brought about by evil or devilish behaviour – wherever it may be, so that healing may begin to take place. When we pray with compassion, we do not wait only for others to be put in our way, for this is only a small part of this particular prayer. For by compassionate prayer, we leave the security of our own existence in order to be with those who are in pain. We do this either by bearing them through our imagination and thoughtfulness into the presence of healing love, or by moving ourselves physically – maybe changing our lives – so that we can live alongside those we have been called to serve in this way.

We should remember also that we who have become immersed in the ocean of the love of God (as we observed in Chapter 8), have also been called to care for creation itself. Just as we cannot divorce ourselves from others, it would also involve a denial of Christ if we were to withdraw our love and concern for the planet. This is not only because human beings need the systems of the earth to work efficiently in order to sustain life but also because the Spirit of God moves in and through them – as he does through us – in order to further his purposes of love. The early Church concluded that the Christ who they described as the visible form of the invisible God (Colossians 1.15) also gave them the way to understand how God, humanity and the world were all caught up in a life that was held together by the Spirit of God. It was through God in Christ that 'all things came into being . . . and without him not one thing came into being' (John 1.3) and 'in him all things hold together' (Colossians 1.17). And Jesus himself says, 'Whoever has seen me has seen the Father . . . Do you not believe that I am in the Father and the Father is in me?' (John 14.9–10). So it is that we find Jesus saying that if we visit and care for others in need, we are caring for him (Matthew 25.45), that God is aware of every bird that falls to the ground (Matthew 10.29) and that he bestows on ordinary flowers a glory that surpasses any glories of wealth, social position and human invention (Matthew 6.28).

Meeting Christ

Compassionate prayer therefore is not a question of caring for others in our prayers so that we might persuade God to help them. It is about recognizing how much God is in all things and all people. To refer to the prayer of compassion as intercession in today's society is often to encourage others to think that it is a way by which we can arrange the best deal possible with God on behalf of those in need. Such an unhelpful approach to compassionate prayer is built on the false assumption that a God of love does not want to help those whose lives have gone wrong. Compassionate prayer is not like calling a friend for help in the middle of the night who eventually helps us only because we have made a nuisance of ourselves (Luke 11.5–8). All we have to do is to ask, search and knock and we will receive, find and the door will be opened. In other words, once we are living and praying within the ocean of love which is the life of God, our lives and his will inevitably coincide, as we saw in the previous chapter. We distort our understanding of the nature of God if we think he can help us simply as a friend or as an earthly parent might respond to our requests (Luke 11.9–14). So wherever our concerns, delights or worthy ambitions lie, love will reveal God to us. St Augustine recommends that when we want to help those who are in need, we should tell them, ' "He is the one we should love. He made the world and he stays close to it." For when he made the world he did not go away and leave it. By him it was created and in him it exists.'[18] For compassionate prayer to be effective, therefore, we have to live sacrificially in the presence of Christ. We may understand this further by looking briefly at the prayer of the Canaanite woman who implored Jesus to help her daughter (Matthew 15.21–28).

Having crossed the border and entered another district, Jesus is confronted by a woman of different nationality who is seeking help for her demon-tormented daughter. We don't know whether the daughter is nearby or at home although we tend to assume the woman is on her own. The story is significant primarily for the discussion that takes place between Jesus and the woman where she seems to persuade him that his ministry is not only for the benefit of the nation of Israel but for everyone. Within this primary aim of the story, concerning the developing ministry of Jesus to those who were not of the Jewish faith, many have noted as significant the way in which the woman asks for help for her daughter. Instead of saying to Jesus, 'Have mercy on my daughter, Lord, Son of David; she is tormented by a devil,' she says, 'Have mercy on me, Lord, Son of David; my daughter is tormented by a demon'. Some might interpret the mother's concentration on her own needs first as selfish. Initially we might think she is asking for help for herself to cope with the trauma of trying to look after and support a daughter who is causing all sorts of problems at home. As we read on, it becomes clear that the purpose of the mother's request is not for herself but for the healing of her daughter. It may be that she asks Jesus first to have mercy on her because in her love and compassion – her sharing of her daughter's suffering – she realizes that her ability to help her daughter largely depends on her own faith and proximity to God. In other words, where the mother is in relation to God can determine to a greater or lesser degree the way or the extent to which God can become active through her in the life of her daughter. She begins by shouting at him from a distance, and the disciples try and persuade him to send her away. How she gets there we don't know, but the woman ends up kneeling in front of Jesus and it is from this place – kneeling before Jesus – that the miracle of healing happens.

If we take this story superficially, we may misunderstand it, just as we misunderstand the story we referred to above concerning the waking of the friend in the night. We might think that healing comes only as a result of persistent prayer, as if God helps us only begrudgingly. But if we look further into the story, we may come to understand another, perhaps deeper, reason why the woman first of all asked Jesus to have mercy on her. She may well have asked for help herself because – although she was a foreigner and maybe of a different faith[19] – she knew that when human beings move closer to God in faith, their love is more likely to become a channel of healing grace.

The Letter of James advises us that there is a vital link between personal holiness and the power of prayer. In this epistle, written perhaps by James the brother of Jesus, and relying heavily on Christ's teaching, we read that 'the prayer of the righteous is powerful and effective' (5.16). Here the prayer of faith which saves the sick and causes the Lord to raise them up (v. 15), should be made by those who have confessed their sins to and prayed for one another that they, too, may be healed. While there may be different interpretations concerning what it means for the sick to be saved and raised up, there is an undoubted link in this, one of the earliest statements written about compassionate prayer, between the faith and life of the person who is praying and the object of their prayers.

I do not want to suggest that the reason why some prayers are not 'answered' is to do with some kind of unconfessed sin, as some would say. As I have already said, to speak too much in terms of God 'answering' prayers is to encourage an unhelpful attitude to prayer based upon consumer needs. It also promotes an anthropomorphic concept of God in the human form of Jesus – except older and with a white rather than a brown or black beard. What James's advice and the woman from Canaan have in common is the understanding that if a prayer is to be authentically Christian, the nearer the person who is doing the praying can be to Christ, the better.

To ask God to have mercy on us before we begin to pray for others is not just to be aware of our need to deal with our unhelpful attitudes towards others that may be preventing us from helping them. It is essentially to pray that we are drawn by God into the presence of God. The Spirit of the universe who inspires our prayers needs sometimes to be given the room within our hearts to unite us to God. The image of the woman kneeling directly in front of Jesus is therefore very helpful. Through her needy devotion, we see both her own strong desire and commitment in prayer as well as her desire for others to know they are caught up in the life of God.

In order to help others to be in touch with God, therefore, we need to be in touch with him ourselves. If we are not in touch – or haven't been in touch for a while – our prayers are likely to be shaped and empowered by desires other than those of eternal love and devotion. They are much more likely to be prayers we use in a form of spiritual combat with God so that he will surrender himself to our requests. Instead, they should be the means whereby we surrender our souls in his mercy to the transforming life of the Spirit. Whether things turn out as we hope or not, these prayers are offered nonetheless, and the objects of our prayers live and die within the life of God. For those who care compassionately for their fellow human beings or for the future of the planet, there can be no better place to live and pray than in the presence of God, even kneeling before the risen Christ. For here we pray as part of creation rather than at or against creation. We seek mercy within the life of God rather than in opposition to it.

We are told that the daughter of the Canaanite woman was healed instantly. We may picture in our minds the demons fleeing from her and leaving her alone at this point. But we are likely to be disappointed if we think of the outcomes of prayer always in terms of results like this. When we are engaged in the processes of divine love, it is usually foolish to look for or expect certain results or outcomes that we have defined for ourselves. Instead, leaving behind the scoreboard of results in terms of what we have achieved or persuaded God to achieve, we might prefer to concentrate on the good that comes about when we follow Christ not only for ourselves but also for others. Rather than pray for life assurance, we ask that his mercies may transform us and others that together we may be carried along by the tide of his love. It is impossible to hate someone we pray for in this way, and the love we are able to bring to bear on others can increase beyond our expectations when it is bathed in compassionate prayer. We pray for those we long to help but who are out of reach – the homeless and those starving in other countries – no longer by ourselves but along with the God of compassionate love, that he will save us and them.

Grounding

Since the very early days of the Church, Christians have used beads or knotted ropes to say prayers. At the end of a service of baptism, I always invite the mother of the child to choose a bead from a box of different coloured and shaped beads, to represent each member of her immediate family. She threads the beads onto a piece of elastic and I then give her a cross to add to what we now refer to as a prayer bracelet. I tie the elastic around her wrist and say a prayer that as the beads are in touch with her so, by her own prayers, she might keep the members of her immediate family in touch with God, as she is in touch with them. I then give her a card on which the following is written:

> By using these prayer beads, you are joining in a long line of Christians in prayer dating back almost to the days of Christ.
>
> We invite you to use these beads – and to wear them on your wrist – to pray for your child who has been baptized today and also for all the members of your family and all those who are closest to your heart.
>
> Each bead represents a member of your family and loved ones.
>
> The cross represents the sacrificial love of God as seen in the life, death and resurrection of Jesus Christ. It can also remind you of the life and witness of the Church of England of which your child is now a baptized member for life.
>
> How to use the prayer beads:
>
> - Simply hold one bead at a time between your thumb and forefinger. As you do so, say a prayer for the person that the bead represents. You can say any prayer you like, one that

you know already or one that you have made up. You might ask God to keep the person safe, or that they may know how much they are loved by you, or that they will be strong if they are facing a particularly challenging day.

- Your prayer can be a sentence long, or longer if you like.
- Move from one bead to the next, praying for each person they represent in turn.
- When you have finished praying, hold the cross and say the Lord's Prayer which Jesus taught his disciples to pray. (You may, if you prefer, say the Lord's Prayer to begin with.)
- You can use this form of prayer anywhere and at any time. You can use it first thing in the morning, on the way to work, when you are out shopping, sitting or kneeling by your child's bedside at night or last thing before you go to bed. You can use the beads once a day or several times during a day. You can use them on your own or with your spouse or partner.
- Sometimes when we are very busy or we cannot find the right words, we can be 'at prayer' by the very act of holding a bead or all the beads together in our hands. As we hold on to them we can remember that God gently holds all of us as his be-loved children in the palm of his hands.
- At the end of the day, you can place the beads by your bedside or over your bed as a sign that you are asking God to watch over you and your family while you sleep.

We hope you enjoy using these prayer beads and that you find them helpful as an aid to prayer.

God bless you and all those who are closest to your heart.

Using the above, you may like to make a prayer bracelet made from elastic and beads or a knotted rope, to help you pray for specific topics or people who may be physically close to you or far away.

Reflecting

If I speak in the tongues of mortals and of angels, but do not have love, I am a noisy gong or a clanging cymbal.

(1 Corinthians 13.1)

Praying

Jesus,
as a foreigner in an alien land,
I kneel before you
and ask that by your mercy
you will heal me and those for whom I pray.
Amen.

10

Prayer and wealth

———◆◆◆———

*Then they arrived at the country of the Gerasenes, which is oppo-
site Galilee. As he stepped out on land, a man of the city who had
demons met him. For a long time he had worn no clothes, and he
did not live in a house but in the tombs.* (*Luke 8.26–27*)

Investing in prayer

Even when we understand the need of compassionate prayer for
all those who suffer, we can end up praying only for those for whom
we can afford to pray. While the nature of compassionate prayer is
to seek out all those in need – without conditions or any kind of
discrimination – and bring them into the presence of the healing
Christ, we can forget that our prayers can be prejudiced by our
finances or the economic structures of the world. For we are brought
up to believe that wealth acquisition is the only real kind of progress
we can make in society and the principal way through which we may
develop.

> We mostly spend those lives conjugating three verbs: to *want*,
> to *have*, and to *do*. Craving, clutching, and fussing, on the
> material, political, social, emotional, intellectual – even on the
> religious – plane, we are kept in perpetual unrest: forgetting
> that none of these verbs have [*sic*] any ultimate significance,
> except in so far as they are transcended by, and included in, the
> fundamental verb, to *be*: and that *being*, not wanting, having
> and doing, is the essence of a spiritual life.[20]

We are surprised sometimes when we realize that, as in all other areas
of the Christian life, there is a cost involved in prayer. Our commitment to the spiritual life is likely to cost us dearly in time as we may
decide we should pray instead of playing golf or going out. There
may also be a cost in terms of our finances when time spent in prayer

is time when we could be earning or increasing our income. Or we may find sometimes that as a consequence of our praying we may become more generous with our money than we might otherwise have been. It may also mean that we have to re-evaluate our lifestyle given our understanding of the significance and worth of others' lives. Living in a society that is very materialistic – where we claim as our right a standard of living way above that which we need, one which is attainable only at the expense of others – it is difficult to pray for those in need around the world. There is a sad irony in praying for the welfare of those whose lives are blighted by poverty when to some extent or other, our wealth and material well-being are founded on – or at least benefit from – their financial need. How do we pray self-righteously, I wonder, for those who perish daily because of the injustices of the economic systems of the world when we ourselves are very much part of the causes of this oppression?

But feelings of guilt will not get us very far. We need to balance our prayers for those in need with actions that bear witness to the love we have for them. Maybe it is because we are aware of the level of institutionalized injustice and know there is very little we can do about it, that we need to pray more earnestly for ourselves and our 'have it all' culture as well as for those who 'don't have it at all'. What is more, we are sometimes less likely to pray for those who compete with us over our claims to the earth's resources, whose growing prosperity may well impoverish us. Why would we want to pray for the successful development of an emerging economy when that nation's growth will produce an increasing population that has to be fed and an industrial growth that will consume precious resources and pollute the atmosphere so as to accelerate the catastrophe of global warming? While such emerging economies represent the faith and fortunes of millions of ordinary people like ourselves, we may feel the need to forget them, or even pray against them, if only so that *we* will survive.

To regard prayer in such terms, or to become consciously or unconsciously exclusive in our prayers, is to work in opposition to the creative energies of life. When we give in to our negative human desires, we subconsciously engage in a form of natural selection when we pray. We may tell ourselves they are of a different faith so have fewer rights to survival. They are the enemies of God, we might suppose. Strangely enough they may think the same of us as they try to secure their promised land for the future.

As we have seen already, we have not been called to pray without love or to claim we have the love of Christ without committing ourselves to the prayer of the universe. For some, prayer involves a world-denying asceticism. This is expressed through the need to lead simple, non-materialistic lives so that our sharing of resources matches our sharing of love for all in prayer and action. But some also take this asceticism to mean that the world itself is somehow evil. In their view, prayer from a position of relative wealth – gained from our engagement with the world – has little to do with God. Some Christians think that having a dishwasher makes you a materialist. But it is only by our deepening engagement with created reality, which includes the society in which we live, that we can unearth the prayer of Christ. We have not been called to prayer from a safe distance but to become involved with the just and unjust structures of society so that we may be agents for change from within. We may feel that much of what makes up our modern society is abhorrent to us. But prayerful engagement with the lives of others means that we have been called to make the prayer of God known wherever human beings are gathered.

So while we might like the idea of opting out of a godless society, we have to force ourselves to live prayerful lives while struggling daily to cope with the excesses that make any kind of spiritual progress an uphill struggle. Otherwise our prayers and our lives are likely to have nothing to do with the kingdom of God. It is only by our deeper awareness of the Spirit of creation, the universal Christ and the God who is in all things that our prayers are caught up in the processes of redemption.

The most effective way in which to ground our prayerful self-offering is through our experience of daily life. We do not save ourselves from the self-interest that largely disregards the needs of others by conducting a pattern of prayer by which we escape – rather than engage in – the life of the world. Having set times of prayer throughout the day – and even the night – can be instrumental in our pursuit of a holy life. But while our praying will necessarily be about our own inward investment, these times of inward journeying should also help to make us more effective in our outward journey in communion with others and with creation. So we have to be careful that our praying does not become a refuge from the harsh realities of life, or a place where we hide from our pain and the fallout of difficult relationships. Others may think we are devout and godly people because we are often at prayer. Yet when our praying becomes a way of escape from pain or fear, what we suppose to be our spiritual wealth is in fact a sign of our poverty. Worse than this, our emotional imbalance, now self-sanctioned by our phoney spirituality, cannot become a channel of healing grace. Instead, as we drape the cloak of our own pretence over others, we distort their understanding of life and drag them into the hell of self-justification.

It is likely that for the foreseeable future those who live in the West will continue to be wealthy in comparison with the majority of human beings on the planet. It is very hard to opt out completely from this. But the Church – within a corrupt and corrupting materialistic society – is called to speak to those who find it abhorrent to live at the expense of others and who feel their prayers suffer as a result. So long as the Church makes an idol of financial security it is unlikely to be seen to engage – or offer others a way to engage – in the prayer of Christ in the world. For this prayer is for the good of all, not just a select few. It is a constant prayer that love, justice and peace will flourish without regard to any financial cost to ourselves or the productivity of those for whom we pray. To those locked into a capitalist mindset, this will appear nothing short of lunacy. But the prayerful pursuit of the kingdom of God revolutionizes human relationships. It does not sit happily alongside economic systems that liberate a few while oppressing the majority. In this sense, the Spirit of Christ calls out to the Church in the West to embrace the world and in so doing embrace him. Instead of embracing human ambition, the Church should speak to it.

The cost of prayer

The story of the way in which Jesus cast demons out of the man of Gerasa is one of the more extraordinary stories in the Gospels. The man, we are told, doesn't wear clothes and has left the city where he once lived. He now lives on his own, not in a house but among tombs, a wild man welcome only among the dead. When his demons take over, he becomes so violent he has to be restrained by chains. Yet such is his strength that even these cannot hold him.

As soon as this demented and dangerous man sees Jesus, he recognizes him as the 'Son of the Most High God'. In his madness, he displays a level of perception that was absent in many of the so-called sane religious leaders of the time, who thought only that Jesus was making insane claims about himself and God.

Realizing his power over them, the demons inside the wild man of the tombs plead that if they have to leave their human host they should be allowed to enter into some nearby animals. A deal is struck and Jesus sends the demons into a herd of pigs that consequently rushes down a steep bank into a lake and drowns.

Generally speaking, we do not believe in demons in the same way as people did in first-century Palestine. While we may find it helpful to describe our negative desires or neuroses as our demons, we are unlikely to give them a personal identity. But if we imagine the confrontation between Jesus and this man, it is likely there would have been raised voices and maybe some shouting – at least from the man who lived in the tombs. Maybe it was the noise that so startled the herd of pigs they ran away, unhappily in this instance to their destruction.

We might think that this is a story with little relevance for any thoughts about the cost of prayer. But there is a salutary warning here for us all, and in particular for the witness of the Church today when many have become impoverished as a result of the greed of others. For if we are not prepared to surrender even our material well-being to God in prayer, we may find that if or when we lose it, we are left with nothing that can comfort us. This is as true for our experience of a financial disaster as it is for our understanding of the way we should approach our life in the hereafter. When, understandably, our personal security is bound up in our faith in financial arrangements, our dialogue with God is likely to become less of a conversation from the heart and more of a transaction about spiritual investment. We lose the currency of love, and our speech is defined by our wealth. When out of our mind with worry, we are more likely to complain to Jesus in prayer about our physical circumstances than to ask for healing for ourselves.

The wild man among the tombs who had lost his home, friends, family and all his possessions admits first that he needs help for himself. Rather than ask for his old life back, he prays – through the demons to whom he has given hospitality – for his peace of mind to be restored. As a consequence, he who was once naked, violent and unpredictable becomes clothed, calm and composed.

You would think that everyone would be happy. But they are not. The herdsmen are understandably very upset, having lost their livelihood. In a country where there was no social welfare programme this would have meant that they would have lost their jobs and the source of income on which they and their families depended. But it is not just the herdsmen who are upset. When they tell the people living in the city and surrounding countryside what has happened, everyone comes out to Jesus and, terrified, they ask him to leave. This is very odd.

Why were they so scared? ('They were seized with great fear', Luke 8.37). Why couldn't they simply give thanks that the wild man was now sane? Why weren't they glad that he wouldn't be living in the tombs any more? Why weren't they pleased that they could visit the final resting place of their relatives without worrying about him jumping out naked from behind a tombstone and shouting at them? Why didn't they react like others had and ask Jesus to stay with them and heal their friends and relatives and those in their own communities who were ill? Why ask him to leave straightaway? To find the answers to these questions, we need to look at the geographical location of this event.

First, Gerasa was on the east bank of the Sea of Galilee, away from Jewish territory. It was a Gentile area under Roman occupation, hence the prominence of the herd of pigs which the Jews considered to be ritually unclean. So it is highly likely that this demon-possessed man and the herdsmen were not Jewish. They were Gerasenes. And while the wild man recognized Jesus as the Son of God, they did not. As far as they were concerned, as we shall see, he was simply a troublemaker.

Second, Gerasa, near the coast, was a thriving and significant trading centre. People came from hundreds of miles away to buy and sell there. And here is the key to the reaction of the people. Just imagine what would happen if word got round that there was a religious extremist in town who in a few words could ruin your livelihood? Think of the disastrous consequences if Jesus used this approach to mental healthcare on the people of the city. Chaos would ensue. Who in the local community or among those who came from far away would risk his livelihood ending up in the lake or some steep ravine? Who would value the life of a demented madman above the source of his income that kept his family fed, housed and clothed? And who would bring his livestock for trading at Gerasa if there was any suggestion someone would destroy them in the name of God? The result of this particular healing miracle therefore is fear. The local population, having invested their lives and livelihoods in the trading centre of Gerasa, could face economic ruin. God's love of humanity was too high a price for them.

So this story of the madman at Gerasa is one of many episodes in the life and teaching of Jesus Christ where his healing love is lost on those who have become rich in the eyes of the world but poor in the eyes of God. They cannot see the goodness that godliness can bring to the human spirit. They live in a society where, through their dependency upon their economic structures, there is no room for God any more. They live in their own little world where their business investments are more important than the salvation of a single human being. They write up their balance sheets at the same time as they write off those who have fallen off the conveyor belt of consumerism. This sounds very familiar and resonates powerfully with the way we live and pray today where we have made a god of cost-effectiveness. We tend not to pray for anything that might put us seriously out of pocket and we forget – almost completely – the priorities of the kingdom where 'there will be more joy in heaven over one sinner who repents than over ninety-nine righteous people who need no repentance' (Luke 15.7).

In addition, we may see from the conversation Jesus has with the wild man and the one he has with the townspeople, how our dialogue with God can be affected by our personal circumstances. In very stark terms, we are shown that when we understand our need of the healing grace of Christ, our prayers draw us into his healing presence. On the other hand, when we feel threatened by the way life is treating us, when we are fed up with the demands God makes on us, or when we re-fashion our image of God according to our material needs, and despite what we consider to be our laudable and appropriate ways of prayer, we will in fact be praying for God to leave us alone. Invariably, as we progress through the spiritual life, we will have opportunities to realign our priorities and interests from worldly concerns to the concerns of the kingdom. As part of this process, we should not be surprised when God asks us – or when we feel it is necessary – to surrender our material possessions if only to make us realize where true wealth lies. When this happens and our instincts tell us to push God away, we should redouble our efforts to become closer to him. In such moments we are likely to have the opportunity to be closer than ever to God provided we are prepared in prayer to admit our need of him.

The most important aspect of this for our prayers, however, is for us to know that when we allow materialism to get in the way, we will not be able to cope with the presence of God in Jesus Christ, even when we pray. And no amount of argument or reasoning or clever words or mission initiatives, advertising, fund-raising projects or stewardship campaigns will make any difference to the life and witness of the Church unless and until by spiritual meltdown, our headlong rush towards economic survival at all costs comes second, at least, to the simple prayer of healing love.

Now, suddenly, this strange story about a deranged and violent man living naked among the tombs retains its power to frighten and condemn those who read it today. For here we are made to realize it is those who build a society based on money rather than on the needs of others, and pray that Christ should leave it alone, who are insane, while those who know their spiritual need of Jesus Christ and pray to be changed are in their right minds.

Grounding

The need to live and pray within a materialistic society – where we claim as our right a standard of living way above that which we need and which comes only at the expense of others – can come at the price of our collusion with what we might feel are godless attitudes towards others. From time to time, we may find it helpful to set a moment aside to reflect on how we can maintain our integrity and identity as Christians. It may be helpful to have a regular discussion about this with others, our spouses, friends, children or soulmates. This could lead us to think about how our prayers are affected by our wealth or poverty and the wealth and poverty of others.

Reflecting

You cannot serve God and wealth.
(Matthew 6.24)

Praying

Almighty God,
in a world where naked ambition
robs others of their rights and dignity,
and gross self-interest
allows many to bleed to death,
grant us the Spirit of your Son
to confront the systems
by which we live at others' expense,
so that we can pray for everyone
to know justice, healing and peace.
Amen.[21]

11

Prayer and poverty

———◆◆◆———

'Truly I tell you, unless you change and become like children, you will never enter the kingdom of heaven.'　　*(Matthew 18.3)*

False assumptions

It is easy to make false assumptions about others. It is usually best not to make assumptions or jump to conclusions at all. I was re-minded of this one day when I made a social visit to an undertakers, as you do sometimes when you are a vicar. During the conversation, we drifted into discussing the smoking habits of a couple of the staff. I suggested we tried to come up with a way to help them kick the habit. I assumed that being involved in the funeral business they would be only too aware of the dangers to their health of smoking, and therefore would naturally want to give it up. Life is short enough as it is. There is no point in making it shorter still. All they needed was a little help from their friends. They told me that because of what they did for a living, they had concluded that, despite the obvious health hazards, there was no point in their giving up smoking. Dealing daily with death had made them want to live life to the full for as long as they could. This was completely the opposite view from what I was expecting. They were very aware that we can spend our time eating healthily and keeping fit, only to be suddenly struck down by an incurable disease or run over while crossing a road. Their approach, therefore, was that they should live life to the full for as long as they could. If they enjoyed smoking, they should carry on enjoying it for as long as possible.

I dare say opinion will be divided over this. There will be those who think smoking is a grossly irresponsible squandering of the quality of life, and an abuse of the body. And there are others who feel everyone has a right to live their life according to their own decisions, so long as they don't adversely affect others. But this is not the place to enter into such a debate – my purpose in telling this story is to highlight my false assumption. I presumed these good people would have avoided anything in their lives that was likely to threaten life. It had not crossed my mind that I would receive the response I did. It was good to have my assumptions challenged by those who held completely different views from my own, whose deepest longing was simply to enjoy the life they have been given.

Just as it is easy to make false assumptions about others, we can also make false assumptions about ourselves and the way we pray. I can remember an occasion early in my ministry when I was asked to lead a workshop on prayer. I duly turned up to the meeting and once the members of the group had introduced themselves and I had introduced the evening's topic, I moved on to the main exercise. I invited everyone present to imagine a scene they could remember from the Bible. Using my imagination like this is something I had done for years. I assumed everyone in the group would be happy to do this. So I was taken aback when a young man in the group inter-rupted me and said that imagining Bible stories was not something he could do. He said he would be happy to write something on paper, draw a picture or make something with his hands, but using his imagination in the way I had suggested was not going to work for him. I had to rethink my plans for the evening very quickly or I would have left this young man out. That evening I learnt that the ways in which people pray and the techniques they use vary enormously. If we are to share anything useful in a practical sense concerning prayer, we have to allow for this. But there are other assumptions we can make with regard to the way we pray, not least those affected by wealth and, in particular, poverty.

We might assume that we who live in comfortable surroundings and do not have to search daily for food and water would have the time and energy to devote to prayer. Rarely thirsty, protected from the rain by a secure roof over our heads, from the wind by double glazing, warmed by central heating and having the benefit of super-market delivery to our doorstep, we can easily find time to pray. Similarly, we might suppose that those who have not been blessed with ready access to the basics of life would not be as inclined to pray; surely their time will be taken up with finding water, making sure the roof and the walls of their dwelling are secure, seeing that the fire remains lit and that food is found for the day. Finding time for prayer and Bible study when your main priority is to survive in a home consisting of one room where all the members of your family relax, eat and sleep must be practically impossible.

On the surface, these may be reasonable assumptions to make. Yet we frequently find them challenged. It is not unusual to discover that those who are well off struggle to find the time to pray. The luxuries that make their lives easier soon become necessities as the pace of their existence accelerates and they attempt to keep up with an increasingly demanding lifestyle. So busy do they become as they try to survive in a highly competitive market place, that it gets more and more difficult to find time for their families and friends and for themselves. Committed to the marketplace of financial survival at such a speed and to such an extent, they become unaware of the need to attribute their wealth and well-being to God. They work hard and, having earned their wealth, consider it their right – and theirs alone – to use it however they want. By contrast, those who face daily hardship, have no regular income and little freedom to decide how they live, may pray constantly throughout the day in their struggle to survive. Prayer forms a natural part of their lives because of the degree to which their lives are earthed in creation. They are acutely aware of drought and flood: their homes can be washed away when all their water comes at once. They are frequently hungry and thirsty. But we who consider ourselves more sophisticated than they are sometimes make terrible assumptions about the simple faith of these people. We can dismiss it almost as primitive superstition. They believe in God because they do not know any better. And, while we do the same, we sometimes criticize them for distorting the teaching of Christ, allowing it to be defined by cultural needs rather than by the cross. Yet their lives and consequently their faith are often caught up in the Spirit of creation much more than they would be if they lived one or two or more steps removed from reality – as we often do – in a cocoon of so-called affluence. When it rains, we stay indoors or travel by car. When it rains, they get wet.

No one should feel guilty about being born into an affluent society. We cannot condemn ourselves as Christians simply because we are wealthy. But, as we saw in the previous chapter, we have to be aware of the corrupting power material wealth can have on our praying. For when we live in a situation where we have all we need – and more – and where we feel we are faithfully contributing to the life of the Church and society, we can mistakenly assume that as a result our praying will be effective and our prayers will be answered. Then, when our prayers do not produce the results we expect, our faith and thanksgiving diminish. We become frustrated that while we make financial transactions every day, we cannot bargain with God in prayer. Yet when those who are poor continue to live in poverty and hardship despite their prayers for a better life, their faith and thanksgiving are undiminished. In this sense, we who are materially well off have much to learn from those who are not. Through our prayers, we need to address the hunger of the soul, become thirsty, welcome the rains and expect our house to be blown down from time to time.

> The Lord said: 'Seek first the kingdom of heaven, and all the rest will be given in addition'. This is our principle, even if the material aspects of life impose themselves on us from morning to night. The world has other goals, and no one has time for prayer any more.[22]

Prayer is even more important now at a time when the economic structures that have underpinned our extravagant way of life have been seen to be more fragile than we ever imagined, not least through their over-exposure to greed and material gain at all costs. If humanity does not embrace the spirit of humility, reorientating itself to the worship of God rather than itself, a hopeless future beckons. Instead of developing a new economics, we shall simply find ways to restore the current system with a few minor adjustments. The Church has all but completely failed to give a lead to society in this respect. Facing financial meltdown for a number of years, it has failed to understand its need as a God-given opportunity to rediscover its identity and meaning through sacrificial love. Instead its leaders and synods have lamentably expended their time and effort in preserving their institutional interests. Having made a god of economic survival at all costs, they have squandered the resources of their faith in a faithless pursuit of self-preservation. At a moment in its history when the Church was given the opportunity to bear the presence of Christ to the world in the simplicity of faith that came from Galilee, it concentrated most of its efforts on 'restoring the current system'. As a result, it has little radical love to offer a society that is now facing a similar challenge. While it will continue to offer institutional security and may well experience something of a renewal as the nation experiences difficult times, its witness is hugely diminished by its continued investment in the markets and priorities of the world. Instead of going out and standing in the rain with those who lack shelter, we have put all our efforts into repairing the roof of a building that is falling down anyway.

Through the life of prayer, every Christian is called to recover the Spirit of Christ through sacrificial love. In this sense, the Church needs to rediscover heartfelt prayer and love. This Christ-like prayer belongs only to those who are prepared to leave the kingdoms of the world behind and rely on nothing but the present moment in the presence of God when they pray. This is the prayer of poverty. By this prayer our lives are caught up in the simplicity of love that redeems humanity's overriding ambition to survive at all costs and at the expense of others. From the powerlessness of this poverty we find the strength to lead a sacrificial life. And the principal way we rediscover this prayer is by learning from those who live in poverty – by choice or necessity – while praying with a clarity of faith we would otherwise struggle to find.

What is more, through this prayer of poverty we leave behind unhelpful assumptions about conditional faith and love and rediscover Christ in the present moment of our conversations with others. Here we seek neither to judge nor condemn but only to love as Christ becomes present in faithful listening and mutual respect, in the open mind and the prayerful heart. By such uncluttered prayerful centredness and devotion we offer and give – without effort and sometimes even awareness – the divine love that makes a difference for good.

The embrace of naked love[23]

On one occasion, his disciples asked Jesus who was the greatest in the kingdom of God. They may have assumed that he would say they were; instead, in response to their question, Jesus called a child forward and told the disciples that unless they changed their way of thinking and became like children, they would not enter the kingdom at all.

It may seem strange that in this instance Jesus refers to a young child. While children of this age may be more open to teaching and guidance about God, what could they possibly know that would gain them entry into the kingdom? A child of this age is unlikely to have achieved the greatness in the service of God that some might think would guarantee it a place in the kingdom. Some feel it is the innocence of the child that Jesus is referring to. Yet, in their innocence, children of this age can be very self-centred and, while delightful, extraordinarily demanding. They do not behave well naturally and are largely governed by their instincts. They have to be taught how to behave and eventually how to love. It is more likely that Jesus told his disciples they had to become like children in order to enter the kingdom of God because children do not own anything. They have no income as such and are too young to have purchased anything. They have no bank account of their own and no investments in the money markets. In this sense children have no vested interests. If you speak to a child about shares, they will think you are talking about sharing what they have been given. Frequently, where children live in poverty, they have to contribute to the well-being of their family in order to survive. While they are very young, they may have to help carry clean water to their home from some distance away, or fuel for the hearth and food for the day. Whatever they have, they are given. They own nothing. They are not paid for what they do. They live with others and, while receiving, also give to others. They contribute to the lives of others while depending entirely on them to support them.

In a similar way we are called to live in the presence of Christ, in poverty of spirit at least, without any vested interests in the wealth of the world where prayer becomes the divine/human embrace of naked love. If we see ourselves as children, we are no longer embarrassed by our nakedness. We come to prayer acknowledging that we do not own anything, understanding life in terms of gift rather than possession and learning how to appreciate and treasure our dependence upon God. Through this prayerful embrace, we embrace the world with the love of Christ. Without it, we fumble around, feeling we are making a difference when we are not, and become a source of embarrassment rather than ambassadors of faith in the world. This prayer of poverty reverses the priorities of the world.

In what we often refer to as Jesus' Sermon on the Mount, he tells the crowds the poor in spirit are blessed, 'for theirs is the kingdom of heaven' (Matthew 5.3). The 'poor in spirit' here are those who live without any dependence upon material things. These words also refer to someone who has decided they no longer have any interest in the false security that can be gained from wealth or power, preferring instead to put their trust in God. Jesus' saying that follows shortly afterwards – that the meek are blessed 'for they will inherit the earth' (Matthew 5.5) – means pretty much the same. The words 'poor in spirit' can also mean 'meek' or 'gentle'. Jesus describes himself in these terms (Matthew 11.29). So those who pursue the prayer of poverty or the prayer of naked love possess the kingdom of heaven while at the same time inheriting the earth. One follows on from the other. So, in the poverty of our prayers, earth and heaven coincide in a way that can change our lives and the lives of those around us. We do not inherit 'lands' or territory and resources we may lay claim to as exclusively our own, given to us by God regardless of the needs of others. Instead we are given the means to become one with the earth and through our earthiness become at the same time one with heaven.

This is the meekness that is central to the meaning of humility (literally being 'of the earth') in the Christian understanding of this term. It is not about being 'meek and mild' in the sense of never speaking above a whisper or holding a strong opinion. It is in our commitment to fulfil this divine embrace of creation and the needs of others that we inherit the kingdom (Matthew 25.34). For faithful living has more to do with a commitment to love than with measuring the success of the Church. 'Inheriting the earth' and 'inheriting the kingdom' in this way come only as a gift of godly insight and openness to the life of his Spirit within us. By using the word 'inherit' here Jesus is making it clear that we come close to God through grace rather than through good deeds. Such closeness is not something we can earn. It is a reward for our prayerful poverty. As we become increasingly aware of our own inheritance of earth – we have come from the earth and we return to it (Genesis 3.19) – we make it available to others. We receive it by being childlike, by our acceptance of our nakedness. We are entirely ourselves, without guile, cynicism or pretence and offer the simplicity of our love and faith to others. The greater our spiritual poverty and our nakedness in prayer, the more likely we are to participate in this life of the kingdom, or eternal life as the evangelist John refers to it.

When visiting an area of significant material poverty in Africa I was struck by the dignity and faith of those who by Western standards had so little. I was invited to a church in a township where a small adult choir was rehearsing for a competition. Their singing was beautiful. Their natural harmonies, arising from their devotion to Christ, had a beauty, freedom and spontaneity not easily found in those places where religion is more formally expressed. I was struck, too, by their dignity and pride. Although they had no access to electricity or washing machines, their clothes were cleaner and better ironed than mine. There was not a trace of that self-pity and resentment that is often found among those in better-off societies who, having fallen on hard times, prefer not to help themselves but instead to blame others. While very poor, the members of this choir were cheerful and faithful and full of self-respect. I was amazed, and began to realize how materialism murders the soul.

These Africans referred to themselves as 'children of the soil'. They had a contentedness, a humility, a simplicity and a godliness that comes from being constantly in touch with the earth, constantly feeling the earth beneath their feet, and the soil between their toes. This is real holiness, a gift that cannot be earned.

I am not saying that all rich people are bad, or that all poor people are good. Nor would I suggest we should not make every effort we can to help the poor. What I know, however, is that the prayer of poverty – or the prayer of the embrace of naked love – is the way we inherit both earth and heaven. I shall never forget the poverty I saw among the townships of Africa, nor at the same time the faith and nobility of spirit found there. I shall always remain profoundly grateful to the people I met for this insight into the kingdom of heaven. I do not wish that anyone anywhere should live in poor conditions, and I am committed like everyone else to the relief of suffering and poverty. But I know that without the challenge of the poor alongside us, we in the developed world would have no chance of redemption. How else may we learn the prayer of poverty? Jesus once told those around him, which included some so-called religious leaders and experts of the time, that they would always have the poor with them (Mark 14.7). He knew that in any human society wealth would inevitably divide people. But instead of gloating about our wealth, we need to learn from the material poverty of others. I feel sure the poor I met in Africa have more life in the kingdom of heaven than I shall ever know. But because of them, I can grow towards this inheritance.

While we pray earnestly for an end to poverty, we know that those of us who are well off in terms of material things can learn from the poor where real wealth lies. It is almost as if the soul of those of us who live in the West – even Western civilization itself – can only be saved by their poverty. For the 'present form of this world is passing away' (1 Corinthians 7.31) and humanity has to move away from the affluence that allows us even to contemplate the squandering of life's gifts through the pursuit of short-term enjoyment. We like to think it is all right to live however we want so long as it does not hurt others, thereby justifying all sorts of behaviour that can not only hurt the body but more importantly the soul as well (Matthew 10.28). In our irresponsible pursuit of pleasure – even in the face of death – we can sometimes forget that whether we live or die, we belong to God (Romans 14.8). The poverty of our prayer, and our commitment to divest ourselves of power and wealth, however, may well lead us to make decisions that upset others. Some may interpret our meekness as a rejection of their values, or assume that our naked love exposes their conditional affection.

While I cannot remember the names of those who sang in that township choir, I have no doubt they will have their reward in heaven, way ahead of me and of all others who refuse to engage in the prayer of poverty.

Grounding

Take some time to go out of your way to be in touch with creation by going for a walk, climbing a hill, looking at a spectacular view or even standing in the rain. Pray for a better understanding of your union with the world and of God's presence within it. Then reflect on how your prayerful meekness can help meet others' needs of God. You may wish to make this exercise a regular feature of your spiritual life.

Reflecting

Whoever becomes humble like this child is the greatest in the kingdom of heaven. (Matthew 18.4)

Praying

Heavenly Father,
in the poverty of our prayer
and the naked embrace of your love,
may we serve you in others
and, inheriting both earth and heaven,
bear witness to the riches
of your grace.
Amen.

12

Prayer and blessing

———◆◆◆———

'Out of the mouths of infants and nursing babies you have pre-
pared praise for yourself.'   *(Matthew 21.16; cf. Psalm 8.2)*

In a word

Some years ago, soon after taking up a post as a vicar of a parish in
Lancaster, I was working in the front garden of the vicarage when a
parishioner passing by on the pavement in front of the house called
out to me. He only said the one word, 'Alright?' I replied that I was
very well and commented on the good weather. I thanked him for
his concern and asked him how he was. Much to my astonishment,
my response obviously took him by surprise. I could see that he had
not been anticipating a lengthy reply or the beginning of a conversation. While he faltered in his step for a moment, he managed to
keep going, concluding what for him had apparently been a tricky
moment.

At the time, I couldn't understand what I had done to cause his
look of surprised anxiety. He had inquired about my well-being and
I had courteously – or so I had thought – responded to his thoughtfulness. What was I meant to do? He surely hadn't expected me to
ignore his greeting? It was a bright summer's morning, all seemed
well with the world and I had appreciated the greeting. What had I
done wrong? It wasn't too long afterwards that I found the answer.
I discovered from a friend about the abbreviated greeting which
said little but meant a great deal. I learned that to say 'Alright?' in
these parts is to say the following in one word: 'Good morning/
afternoon/evening. It's very good to see you. How are you and your
family? I hope you are well. If there's anything I can do to help you,
please let me know. Have a good day.' The reply which contains the
same sentiments: 'Good morning/afternoon/evening. It's good to

see you, too. I hope you and your family are all thriving and that you have a good day as well. If there is anything I can do for you, please let me know' is also summed up in the repetition of the one word, 'Alright?'

Across Lancaster at least, therefore, there are lengthy greetings and expressions of care and comfort being conducted all the time in the briefest of conversations. Greeting: 'Alright?' Response: 'Alright?' If nothing else is said, both parties presume everything is 'alright'.

I do not know the origin of this but there are similar short, coded greetings used in other parts of the country. The other day when I visited another part of the country a man greeted me by saying, 'Alright, me duck'. On this occasion, it was my turn to feel surprised anxiety and the desire to keep on walking. I suppose it was much easier to say, 'Alright' and contain a whole conversation concerning the well-being of another person in a word, if you were working in a noisy mill where conversations were a waste of time because nobody could hear what anyone else was saying. Today, when we are constantly looking for ways to save time in a fast-moving society, one-word greetings that say so much can be very useful. It occurred to me that instead of preaching for ten minutes on a Sunday morning, I should just get up and say, 'In the name of the Father and of the Son and of the Holy Spirit. Alright?' and everyone in the congregation would respond, 'Alright?' We could then proceed to share the Peace with one another, 'Alright?' 'Alright?' The service consequently would be shorter and we could all be home with plenty of time to read the newspaper, play with the children, wash the car, mow the lawn, nip down to the pub for a pint and take the dog for a walk, all before lunch. Alright.

More recently I have noticed another abbreviation of sentiments which is most common among young mothers. When their child – or someone else's – does something charming or cute, the mums will sometimes say, 'Ah, bless' or just 'Bless'. This really means something like, 'Look at little Sarah. Isn't she cute the way she has dressed up the cat in the baby's bonnet?' The word, 'bless' is also used as an expression of sympathy for children or adults. 'Have you heard that Robert's not well? He's had such a tough time recently and while we thought he was getting better, his illness seems to have returned.' 'No, I hadn't heard about that. Ah, bless,' comes the reply, meaning 'I am so sorry that Robert is unwell again. He seems to be having a tough time. I do hope he receives the support he needs and feels better soon.'

So today when we use the word 'bless' – as in the example of the little child – it is sometimes because we want to express our joy and appreciation because of something someone has done, or simply as an expression of our love and affection for them. Or we may use this word to say we hope someone who is in distress receives all the help they need and that the God of creation brings whatever super-natural support that might be available to their aid. In these usages at least, blessing others becomes a normal part of daily life. In this sense, anyone can bless someone else. This includes those who have a strong Christian faith and those who do not.

By contrast, in the traditions and practice of the Church of England, only priests are allowed to pronounce a formal prayer of blessing on behalf of the Church. This often takes place at the end of a service so that those assembled leave the church and go out into the world empowered and supported by the blessing of God. Children – and sometimes adults – who have not been confirmed come to the altar rail for a blessing during the administration of the bread and wine of Holy Communion. A blessing is given instead of the bread and wine until they have been through a course of instruction concerning their membership of the Church and the meaning of Communion. This blessing is given as a prayer of hope for the future, or perhaps as a prayer that reveals Christ's presence in a special way or as a way to justify the nonsense that a person is welcome to receive the life of Christ but not yet.

So there are many different ways in which we express blessing for one another. There is the everyday expression of love and care that is uttered without formula or restriction. It comes naturally to the lips of those who love and care and maybe also wish to commend others to God. And there are also the set prayers of blessing of the Church. These formal prayers are different from the everyday bless-ings not least because the priest blesses others in the name of God on behalf and with the authority of the Church she or he represents. Yet there are those who somehow feel that a priest's blessing 'works' in a spiritual way that is different from the blessing of a mother or father for their children. Maybe this is because they consider the life of the priest to be one that has been particularly dedicated to prayer and the spiritual life, or simply because a priest comes with the authority of the Church. Therefore, when a priest says a prayer of blessing, it is often perceived to have more spiritual clout than the blessings of others who do not have the same opportunities to be about God's house of prayer.

It is certainly true for many that the blessing of the parish priest on special occasions – both of joy and sadness – retains a special significance which is usually much appreciated. It is an enormous privilege to be asked to bless a newborn child, to say a prayer of blessing for a family in need, or to bless someone's new home, for example. But for some – both within and outside the church – who ask for and receive such blessings, a supernatural element has crept into their understanding of what is going on. It is almost as if there is an unspoken residual awareness among them that when a priest says a blessing 'something happens' in terms of something almost 'magical'. Yet, while it is used in a number of different ways, this is not how the verb 'to bless' is used in the Bible or in stories of the life of Jesus Christ. The word the writers of the New Testament mostly used for 'bless' means literally 'to speak well of' in the sense of praising someone or wishing them happiness and prosperity. They also used it to describe the consecration of someone or a special object to be set aside for God.

Out of the mouths of babes

We frequently struggle to be authentic in our praying when we assume adult independence, as it is easy to be caught up in selfish ambitions and self-importance. Prayerful union with the divine energy of creation becomes almost impossible when we keep the Spirit of creative love at arm's length in this way. Secretly, we prefer to shake hands with God as equals in an act of self-justification rather than surrender ourselves to the embrace of naked love. In the previous chapter, we noted the significance of childlike identity as a way to understand our relationship with God and to enter the kingdom by praying to him as Father. As children we cannot pray from a position of false power and influence, assuming property rights and vested interests in the kingdom. But although we think of ourselves as children, we do not pray in that frame of mind that reduces our ability to think for ourselves, or which would make us helplessly dependent on God. As children, we take responsibility for our lives while at the same time acknowledging our need of the God who as the creator and sustainer of the universe provides the stability we need for an ordered existence.

When visiting the Temple in Jerusalem, Jesus was horrified by its commercialism. Vested interests had taken over to such an extent that there was no room for childlike faith. Devotion to God was defined through a rigid assertion of national identity and a promotion of religious purity that had become the exclusive preserve of those who obeyed the rules and paid the admission fee. Jesus had hoped to find a prayerfulness that was authentic in its self-abandonment to God. Instead, he discovered a degree of vested interest so great that it prevented rather than promoted the blessing of those who entered.

Jesus makes it clear that materialism and personal financial gain inhibit rather than promote the process of prayer. So he upsets the powerful religious leaders while attracting the powerless ordinary folk. Ordinary people with childlike faith, stumbling and limping their way through life – like so many of us – discover in Jesus something they could not find in the formal religion of high walls and exclusive piety. They experience the presence of God in Jesus who engages with the world while at the same time reminding them – their minds were renewed (Romans 12.2) – of heaven. Their hopes and dreams for stability and prosperity are blessed by him in a way they have not come across before. Jesus is able to help these people to see life in a new way and to walk without pain because they know their need of him and want the blessing he can give. But when those who throng around Jesus in the Temple suggest he has a religious identity and authority that comes directly from God, the authorities become angry and accuse him of godlessness. Matthew (21.14–16) describes the scene as follows:

> The blind and the lame came to him in the temple, and he cured them. But when the chief priests and the scribes saw the amazing things that he did, and heard the children crying out in the temple, 'Hosanna to the Son of David', they became angry and said to him, 'Do you hear what these are saying?'

Rather than engage in theological debate, Jesus focuses his accusers' attention on the children in the Temple. He reminds the chief priests and scribes of a verse from a psalm they would have known very well. He says, ' "Yes; have you never read, 'Out of the mouths of infants and nursing babies you have prepared praise for yourself?' " '

(Matthew 21.16, quoting Psalm 8.2). We might assume Jesus is referring to the infants around him who are making an unseemly noise
in the Temple as they rush about in their excitement. More likely, the
words 'the children crying out in the temple' refer to the same blind
and lame people who had come to him to be healed. Jesus is not
referring to another group of children whose presence we had not
been aware of until this point. These are words that have been very
carefully recorded for the prayer of the early Church. In the presence
of those who claimed maturity in faith – the chief priests and
scribes – and in the heart of their religious establishment where an
over-investment in the politics of power had all but obliterated the
presence of prayer, Jesus restores the meaning and purpose of prayer.
He says that those who can offer praise to God are only those who
are prepared and willing to come to him as children in faith. He is
referring not only to the prayers of the young but also and especially
to those of the grown-ups who through childlike prayer bring blessing to God by their praise. And praise is nothing if not the way humans
speak well of God. So, in their weakness and powerlessness these
adults had found that as children in faith, they had the insight to recognize the presence of God. Those who presume they are too grown
up for such behaviour and faith cannot see him for who he is.

Only when as children of God we worship in this way can we then
become involved in a relationship of mutual blessing through which
we as children bless God as he blesses us and the world. We might
want to add that once we have become the children of God, we can
do no other than speak well of him. In the final chapter of Luke's
Gospel, the risen Christ remains unrecognized by two of his followers until the moment when they are resting from a day's journey
and he breaks bread and blesses it at table. Following the death of
Jesus, these disciples – who in all likelihood had been present in the
Temple on the occasion we are discussing – had turned their backs
on Jerusalem. Over the previous week, sacrificial religious rite had
desensitized them to the extent that they doubted the existence of
divine love. Now, as Jesus breaks and blesses the bread, their eyes
are reopened to the possibilities of the divine life in creation. As
they recognize the presence of Christ with them on what will have
been one of the most difficult journeys they will ever have made, they
find themselves transformed and their understanding of creation
changed. They immediately retrace their steps to Jerusalem. In the

end, Luke tells us that Jesus led the disciples out of the city and took them to Bethany where, while lifting up his hands and blessing the disciples (literally 'speaking well of them'), he was carried up to heaven. Afterwards, the disciples return to Jerusalem where they are continually blessing ('speaking well of') God.

So, the prayer of love is the prayer of the blessing of creation. Jesus 'speaks well of' the bread, as God has chosen this prayerful act to satiate the spiritual hunger of the world. Through our prayers of blessing we seek to receive the food through which we find eternity (John 6.58). And, from the blessing of the bread, we understand that in a wider sense, our use or abuse of creation can bring both blessing and curse to us. While God blesses us through creation, he does this also and especially through Jesus. Luke provides us with a final image of Jesus blessing his disciples as he left them. It is as if we are being offered a glimpse of the life of Jesus in heaven, whose purpose now is to sing our praise, to bless us, not least through our growing understanding of the life of his Spirit. And there is a sense in which all our prayers 'speak well of God' and bring blessing to him because they arise out of our loving response to him. To admit our love for God is to speak well of him in all circumstances as he speaks well of us. And by the mutual blessing of divine dialogue – the continuous prayer of love in our hearts – our lives bring blessing to others. This occurs not because we are engaged in casting magic spells or because we are considered to be deeply religious people, but because as children we engage in the language of prayer that is the embrace of love uniting heaven and earth.

Those who may not refer to themselves as committed Christians also join in this blessing of the world as by 'speaking well of others' they are caught up in the blessing of life that comes from divine love. To enquire after someone's well-being, if only to ask them if they are 'alright', is to be a part of the language of blessing that is revealed most clearly in the Word of God made flesh, Jesus Christ. At a time when we can be very careless of the way we speak, we would perhaps benefit from reminding ourselves from time to time of the blessing that comes from prayerful dialogue. Those who prefer to live behind the high walls of formal religion today may be surprised when the children of the earth – through whom God blesses creation – are not found exclusively to be within the portals of their institutional interests.

Jesus reminded his followers that it is by this prayerful blessing of the Father for his children and the children of the Father – more than all the worthy religious practices we can offer – that others are drawn into his embrace: 'Whoever welcomes one such child in my name welcomes me' (Matthew 18.5).

Our church buildings – our houses of prayer today – are set aside so that, beyond the forms and formularies of prescribed relationships, they may be places where prayerful blessing enriches the hearts of human beings. At one time we may have thought God cursed us. Now we know he speaks well of us as we speak well of him through our prayerful lives. And if he speaks well of us, we should speak well of one another whether we are in church, at home or simply passing the time of day with others.

We are often reminded that we should count our blessings. When we speak ill of others, we are not blessed at all, for we have ceased to pray for them. But by speaking well of others in heartfelt prayer in the conversation of our lives, we share God's blessing with them. St Paul encourages us as follows:

> Bless those who persecute you; bless and do not curse them. Rejoice with those who rejoice, weep with those who weep. Live in harmony with one another; do not be haughty, but associate with the lowly; do not claim to be wiser than you are. Do not repay anyone evil for evil, but take thought for what is noble in the sight of all. If it is possible, so far as it depends on you, live peaceably with all. (Romans 12.14–18)

These are words of blessing for our society where we are often very critical of one another and cause untold hurt and offence by what we say. When the language of blessing is absent, many curse the light as if it is the night and the night because it is not the day. To join in the prayer of blessing, in a world where many disorientated souls live only for themselves within a violent desecration of human being, is to pray for the redemption of the world in the language of heaven.

Grounding

You may like to consider ways in which your prayers may be helped by considering your thoughts and words in terms of the language of blessing. You may also consider how you may develop your practice of speaking well of others in prayer and in daily life. You may be aware that you do not speak well of everyone.

Reflecting

Blessed be the God and Father of our Lord Jesus Christ, who has blessed us in Christ with every spiritual blessing in the heavenly places, just as he chose us in Christ before the foundation of the world to be holy and blameless before him in love.

(Ephesians 1.3–4)

Praying

Father God
May I speak well of you
as you speak well of me
that by prayerful conversation
my life will be a blessing
to a broken world.
Amen.

Part 4

THE PRAYER OF STILLNESS

Forethought

There are many different ways to pray. The secret of an effective prayer life is to find an authentic way of prayer that suits us as individuals, and to ground that prayer completely in love.

Traditional ways of praying do not suit everyone, nor do the common liturgical expressions of prayer we come across in corporate Sunday worship. These sometimes touch our hearts as we are drawn in to the communion of other people at prayer, but often we can be left feeling that we have been little more than spectators. We pray because the minister invites us to, but we may not be sure exactly what we are doing or why. So we sometimes feel we would like to change the words of the man who said to Jesus, 'I believe; help my lack of belief' (cf. Mark 9.24) to 'I pray, help my lack of prayer.'

It is good – even essential – to spend time looking at the way we pray and asking ourselves whether this is the only or the most appropriate way of praying for us at this time. Maybe our prayerful contribution to our structured services of worship on Sundays would be better understood if we could better understand or develop the way we pray during the week.

The Prayer of Stillness is a way that can help us reassess and even renew our times of personal prayer, providing maybe a different perspective on what we are meant to be doing – or not doing – when we pray.

As we shall see, all prayer requires both commitment and love. With both of these, prayer can become exciting and invigorating and while often regarded as the hard work of the Christian life and ministry, we need never feel for long that we have allowed our prayer life to become disengaged from who we are or where we are.

The chapters that follow concerning prayer and work are included because for prayer to develop we need to try to get rid of all false expectations about what prayer is and what prayer can 'do' for us. We need also to let go of all false and unhelpful expectations of ourselves in prayer, for these expectations are usually unreasonable and can quickly reduce us to the false status of incompetent failure.

13

Does prayer work?

We like things to 'work'. We want them to function as we expect them to, and usually for our benefit. Most of us become frustrated when things we expect to 'work' in a particular way don't function as we hope they will. The television may break down just as we are about to watch a long-awaited programme. When this happens, we have to make do with some other activity – reading a book, going out to the pub or for a walk, catching up with odd jobs at home – until the television has been repaired. If we are fortunate, we may possess two (or more) televisions. In this case we either change rooms or move a television. We still might feel frustrated, though, because our second television is not as good as the one that is broken; the screen may be smaller, the picture less clear.

There are other pieces of equipment that need to function in our daily lives. Watching television may be part of our recreation but when things that we need for daily life or our work go wrong, the frustration can be more keenly felt. A computer may malfunction, meaning that we cannot work or retrieve vital information for a while. The telephone line may go down, so that we cannot access the Internet. The bus or train may not run on time, making us late for work. But the frustration we feel at these times is only temporary. By calling in help from others, the situation can usually be rectified – the problem solved – in a short period of time. Soon we are back on track again and feeling a certain amount of control over our lives, or at least those aspects of our days where we need to be able to function fairly efficiently.

When, however, we come to what we call our 'spiritual life', of which praying is a central part, the normal laws and rules that govern our behaviour and by which we create order are often fairly distorted and, in our busy lives, no longer seem to apply. But, at least subconsciously, we assume they ought to.

We express a kind of faith every time we get into a car and put the key in the ignition before driving away. This faith comes from our knowledge that the car is in good working order, is reliable and will function in a specific, predictable manner under our guidance and direction. While, of course, we do not think of God as some kind of fantastic machine – although some of us do seem to project divine-like qualities on our cars and on some other material benefits of our existence – we can nevertheless apply the same kind of laws and expectations to God as we would to day-to-day practical matters. Our faith in God comes from our knowledge – handed down over many centuries – that God is in good working order.

We have an inherited formula from which we make assumptions about how God should act and react in any given situation. The formula is:

- God is essentially a God of love.
- He has omnipotent power, therefore we can rely on him completely.
- He created the world and is actively working within it.
- He loves everyone and wants them to flourish.
- As a loving parent, he is always there for us.

However, we soon discover that when we pray, and particularly when we ask for help, God does not function in a specific, predictable manner under our guidance and direction, or according to our set of maker's instructions for constructing a God who will be on our side.

When we feel this particular frustration in prayer, we can react in a number of ways. We may invent all manner of schemes and reasons why God has not 'performed' for us. We can become adept at selecting passages from the Bible to prove our point. We convince ourselves that our prayer hasn't 'worked' because there is some area of unconfessed sin in our lives that is blocking God's communication with us. The spiritual fuel pipe has become blocked with some kind of polluting debris and needs a clear-out. Another invention of frustrated faith in prayer is to kid ourselves that we haven't used the right words or the correct formula to turn God on. Maybe we used someone else's prayer when we should have used our own. Or perhaps we should have used someone else's words rather than our own.

The common feature of these and many other inventions is the assumption that for some reason – unknown to us and known only to God – our prayer has not 'worked'. Of course, this is nonsense. Nothing of the kind has occurred. The prayer for healing, or strength or peace or insight or love has not 'worked' because God doesn't 'work' according to the principles of mechanics, of cause and effect, in any predictable, proportionate or measurable way.

We believe that God is essentially a God of love, but we forget that love – authentic love rather than the emotional or self-gratifying kind – is both unpredictable and uncontrollable. Authentic love will find its own way, and reach its own level and will always frustrate us and happily surprise us because it does not conform to our needs and expectations.

Love has its own and complete way in the life of Jesus. And one of the exciting and frustrating aspects of the lives of those who lived with him and who were constantly in his company was his complete unpredictability. He did not conform to any of the usual stereotypes either of human or divine behaviour. You could never predict what he was going to say, where he was going to go or what he was likely to do. He turned life upside down. And when you needed him most of all to be strong for you and to be there for you, he allowed himself to be taken away and left you to it.

After many years I have come to the conclusion, therefore, that when we expect prayer to 'work' we are often guilty of making two crucial errors:

1 We subconsciously apply the laws of mechanics rather than the way of love to our relationship with God.
2 We assume we know God well enough to control him, or at least to be able to predict what he is going to do or what he ought to do.

Given this, it can be helpful to remind ourselves that prayer does 'work' but not in the way we usually expect or think we understand.

There are times when I have prayed for guidance and felt I have received it, and there are times when I have prayed for physical healing for others and it hasn't happened. Yet I firmly believe that all the prayers I have said have been 'answered'.

The easy, rather naive and spiritually lazy way to justify this is to say that when I think God has not answered my prayer, he has in fact answered it but not in the way I had expected. This kind of thinking fails to answer the question about unanswered prayer because it still applies the logic of measured cause and effect, of worldly criteria, to the One who is beyond – way beyond – such pre-determined patterns of behaviour.

Instead, I have come to the conclusion that prayer 'works' and all my prayers have been 'answered' for as long as I have lived within the love of God. This is not due to any merit of my own but is instead to do with how I have been created – along with everyone else – within the loving processes or, to put it another way, within the heart of God.

My life is part of the divine life of this creation, and so I cannot think or do or pray anything without it affecting the source and sum of love and life which is God himself. Unless, of course, I choose to absent myself from his company. Should I do this, life will mean even less and my contribution to it is likely to be demonically chaotic. That is why the only sin that cannot be forgiven is the sin against the Holy Spirit (Matthew 12.32), the denial of the love of God. I am likely to make a mess of my life many times over, but it only becomes a meaningless and formless chaos when I refuse to allow the refreshing and re-creating wind of the Spirit to blow over it (Genesis 1.2).

They say that when a butterfly flaps its wings in an Amazonian rainforest it will have a direct bearing on the weather in the United kingdom. So my life lives within the breeze or breath of the Spirit that embraces my soul, bringing me closer to God and to his creation.

And that is as far as I need to go. Any further and I, too, shall be in danger of cutting God down to a size that fits all. Or, to put it another way, I shall be guilty of making God in the image of humanity.

So, prayer is to do with relationship, and prayer – our 'conversation' with God and his 'conversation' with us – reflects the limitless extent to which neither of us can do anything without affecting the other.

So, to engage in prayer is never a futile exercise. It is an embrace of love. It is never a waste of time. It is an expression of the love of God in our hearts, and our love in the heart of God. It always has an effect. And it affects me and my relationships with others as it affects God. This is the God who knows the secrets of our hearts (Romans 2.16) and, as the psalmist reminds us, there is nowhere in earth or under the earth or in heaven where we can be apart from him (Psalm 139.7–12).

14

Prayer is hard work

If prayer can affect our lives and move us on with God, we feel it makes sense to believe that by prayer we can help others to move on with God as well.

The Church has a long history of intercessory prayer which is based upon the life and teaching of Jesus Christ. This kind of praying can be traced to a much earlier time in Christianity's antecedent history in the Jewish faith. There is not the time here to go into much detail about this, suffice it to say that looking through our historic traditions concerning the way we have approached God and sought his assistance for ourselves and for others, we can see that intercession – praying to God on behalf of others – has always been central to our spiritual life, developing its nature and intensity over the years.

In some ways, it may feel as if interceding for others leads to frustration for similar reasons to the ones I have already mentioned. We pray for others to recover from sickness, and their condition worsens – so we, quite naturally, doubt whether God has heard the prayer, wonder whether there is something wrong with us, the intercessors, or even whether intercessory prayer can be said today to 'work' at all any more.

Simply because this is such a substantial subject, I don't intend to say much about it here, and hope that what I have already said and what follows will encourage the reader sufficiently to continue to pray for others. In some ways, though, we cannot help feeling from time to time that our experience of praying should be easier than it is. Once again our logic and reason inform us that if God is love, and Jesus Christ taught us to pray both for ourselves and for others, it should be a relatively straightforward task. God is on our side and has asked us to do this, so how can we lose? Well, the answer often is, 'All too easily.'

We can also say that for a lot of people – many of whom may be unclear about their belief in God – prayer comes naturally. Even the most agnostic people revert to prayer instinctively when they find themselves in a time of crisis. How often have we – and many, many others who would not necessarily describe themselves as religious people – been driven to our most earnest and fervent prayer when we have been in serious difficulty. 'Do this for me, God' or 'Help me with this' or 'Get me out of this', we pray, 'and I'll never let you down again and I'll become a totally devoted follower of yours for the rest of my life.'

Unfortunately, for the development of our self-understanding and the growth of our spiritual life, as soon as the crisis is over, we tend to forget our promises and revert to living in a way that to a greater or lesser degree is independent of God. Some would argue that the reason why we react in this way is to do with our primitive instincts. In the history of the spiritual development of humanity, it has been instinctive to call out to a greater power than ourselves when a crisis has threatened us or our loved ones or our friends or members of our group or tribe.

It is up to our own powers of spiritual discernment and faith as to whether we believe that God has helped or refused to help us once the crisis has passed; yet, whatever conclusion we reach, we can surprise ourselves by how quickly we revert to this kind of mindset later when we find ourselves in similar circumstances.

You could also say that praying comes naturally because there is God in all of us and it is the Spirit of that God who overrides our logic and reason when situations threaten to overwhelm us. It is natural or instinctive to intercede for others because at a subconscious level that which is of the nature of God within us calls out to the God we also perceive as being above and beyond. While we cannot prove it, we feel that this largely unconscious relatedness with God is a sign or a mark that we have been made in the image of God. We suppose that we are living apart from him, yet are surprised on occasions at how close we are to him and he to us. St Augustine once famously said he thought that God is closer to us than we are to ourselves.

So, calling out to God for ourselves when we are in great need and for others when they are in need can be considered a natural thing to do. But if it is natural, why is it often such hard work?

While some seem to find prayer relatively straightforward, the experience of many is that while there are times when it is easier to pray or when prayer comes more naturally, for much of the time it is all we can do to make time to sit in an armchair for a couple of minutes each day to pray. We can at least take some comfort here from the knowledge that periodically every saint or spiritual teacher has, at some time or other, found prayer hard going.

One of the principal reasons for our experience of the difficulty of praying is that we simply just don't have – or find it extremely difficult to find – the time. The familiar adage, 'If you are too busy to pray, you are too busy' makes sense until you try and use it to redeem your prayer life.

Competing demands that often drain us of our emotional and physical energy deprive us of the right frame of mind we need in order to pray. Work, children, relatives, shopping and so on can all crowd out our own needs in what we might have anticipated was going to be one of our easier days. Add to this the speed at which life takes place around us, accelerated by the revolution in communications and information technology, and we end up screaming that for God's sake we want time – quality time – for ourselves, let alone additional quality time with God.

As a result of many new resolutions, we might finally chisel out a few quiet moments in the day to be still, reflect and pray, knowing that if for any reason we miss this opportunity, it is unlikely that we shall be able to recapture it later on. Because such moments are rare, it is helpful to develop ways of praying in among the daily demands of our sometimes complex and crazy existence. The early Celtic Christian communities were particularly adept at this. Whether you were in a monastery or living elsewhere in community, you had prayers that took you through the day. There were prayers for lighting fires, drawing water, preparing meals and so on. The Orthodox Church too has this tradition within its spirituality. In the Latin West later on it was St Benedict who encouraged his followers always to say a prayer before beginning any task, and Brother Lawrence is also known for his prayer while washing up the pots and pans in his monastery.

We struggle to observe this prayerful attentiveness to everyday tasks, and our relationship with God is often quite institutionalized and concentrated on Sundays and specific Christian gatherings during the week. We find it difficult, too, to build into our lives the quiet time for prayerful reflection which is crucial to the stability of many – though not all – Christians, and we forget the prayer that is grounded in everyday things and everyday life.

It doesn't help either that, in the West in particular, we have to a great extent intellectualized our praying. Precise thoughts and words figure too prominently, and our overactivity spills into our prayers. We 'do' prayer rather than 'be' prayer. Again it was St Augustine who said that our hearts are restless until they find their rest in God; yet even when the committed Christian prays, it is often a struggle to get in touch with that deep spiritual restfulness where we can be most deeply in touch with God.

The followers of Jesus were first known as 'followers of the Way', and prayer becomes more possible when our faith develops into a 'Way of life'. This is a way of living a deeper and different kind of life while remaining in a fairly superficial and monochrome Western society. Prayer is often hard work, therefore, because we restrict ourselves to specific times and words without allowing the Spirit to join these times together by other wordless prayers and actions throughout the day.

The traditional monastic routine of the Liturgy of the Hours, of saying prayers at set times of the day and night, was not simply a way of making people stop what they were doing and return to God, thus orientating the day and ultimately one's life around God. It was also – and continues to be – a reminder of that other, hidden, ongoing and unceasing prayer of the Holy Spirit in the heart of the believer and the universe that is constantly beating in time with the heart of God.

There are other reasons why prayer can be hard work, but we don't have space to go into them here. Suffice it to say that when we experience this hard work, we are not the first nor are we likely to be the last to feel this way. In fact, far from thinking that our difficulties in praying prove the weakness of our faith, we should instead understand that this problem brings us into the community of many saints and godly people with whom we share both great Christian happiness and hard labour.

15

The work of prayer

The work of prayer is essentially a labour of love. This is not to suggest that when we pray we should necessarily feel love for God, for ourselves and for those for whom we are praying. While love can affect the way we feel, it does not depend upon how we are feeling at any one time. Nor is love defined by our emotional equilibrium. For love is about commitment as much as anything else.

The Bible is divided into two main sections: the Old Testament and the New Testament. In very general terms these could also be called 'The Old Commitment between God and the people of Israel founded upon the law' and 'The New Commitment between God and the world founded upon love'.[24] And it is interesting that sometimes today in human relationships, law precedes love. In fact, you could argue that you never really have the security or freedom to love before you have established an external, legal kind of framework for your relationship.

We fall in love and become sometimes almost overwhelmed by how we feel for another person to the extent that we feel we cannot live without them. We need them for our lives to make sense. And if they feel the same way about us, we can agree to be married and become legally bound to one another. Untying this legal bond is never straightforward although some will find it quicker and easier than others. The legal bond or framework – feared and misunderstood by many as something that can only tie down and inhibit – provides a personal and public contract of lifelong commitment between two people on which they will base their lives.

The legal marriage agreement will be largely forgotten most of the time, for as the love grows and deepens, it provides the driving energy of the partnership. Only when the relationship goes through a difficult time – as most do at some stage or other – will one or both partners remind themselves and one another of their contractual agreement. Contrary to much popular myth-making, this is where true love thrives. There is no such thing as free love, as there is no love that does not demand much of us as we gradually come to terms with ourselves in relation to others.

As we learn increasingly about the nature of love and how it operates in relationships, we are often surprised by what we come across. The emotions that overwhelmed us to begin with can persist and resurface from time to time. Sometimes these feelings change. They become somehow even deeper and less dependent on whether we are having a good or a bad day.

While all this is going on, we learn new skills which at one time we would not have readily associated with love. Whereas we might at first have thought of one day 'growing old' together, we now think of how we are constantly 'growing up' together. Once we thought we knew how best to support one another, but now we realize that support that in any way supplants someone else's ideas, thoughts or freedom with our own solutions – what we think it is right for them to do – can subtract rather than add to the health and happiness of the one to whom we are devoted.

Most of the time, all we can do is to 'be there' for them as best we can. What is important here, though, is that *we* are there for them. *We* rather than someone else. We know them better than anyone else and we are the ones who have committed ourselves to be with them.

So love can never be measured by our emotions, nor strangely enough does it depend upon how good we are at solving the problems of someone else. Nor does it depend upon how good we feel the relationship is at any one time. There are times when we can feel much love for someone and there are equally times when we think we feel very little for them at all. But even or especially in these times, we can still say we love them in the sense that they ultimately are the ones with whom we share a commitment to try and make as much sense as possible of our lives . . . for better or worse.

A life of prayer that is based upon a contract of committed love can therefore be described as a labour of love. And we commit ourselves to prayer regardless of our emotional highs and lows and, more importantly, regardless of how we think our relationship is going. For we can no longer think of prayer in terms of 'growing old' with God. Prayer is not simply a source of spiritual warmth and comfort to get us through the different stages of life. If it becomes only this, we will have reduced it to the level of some kind of spiritual central heating designed to keep us warm on cold winter nights.

The labour of prayer instead beckons us to grow up with God – constantly. Or in other words, to own our inheritance in Christ by the life of his Spirit in us (Ephesians 1.14) and continue to live our lives in him 'rooted and built up in him and established in the faith' (Colossians 2.7). This transformation takes place as we wrestle with ourselves to pray and to make sense of prayer.

The labour of prayer also involves the sometimes uncomfortable understanding that whereas we think prayer is principally about getting God to do things for us, it is usually more to do with the way in which God helps us to look after ourselves. An omnipotent God who overrules our wills and the calamities we cause for ourselves and others will be an overbearing presence that crushes our individuality. On the other hand, a God who waits for us, is endlessly patient, who desires that we should take responsibility for how we are, who helps us make our own decisions and find our own solutions, is one who celebrates our individuality and semi-independence within the covenantal bond of love.

Sometimes we can become perplexed by the way in which settling down in a contractual relationship with another person can take away the 'shine' or romance of the original meeting and falling in love. The spirit of joy can on occasions be stifled by the slog of daily routine. We can also be confused by the way in which our attempt to live a life of prayer can make our life more, rather than less, complicated. We can be forgiven if at times we think we would have been better off if we hadn't bothered with the idea of being Christian. It is when the labour becomes this intense that we need to look at the way in which we pray.

It is likely that we will pray in different styles and with differing degrees of understanding as we grow in faith and grow up in our understanding of and relationship with God. There will be some times when prayer comes more easily and others when it is the last thing we feel we want to do or have time to do. There will be occasions when we can achieve a high degree of self-discipline and observe set times of daily prayer or quiet times. And there will be days or weeks or even months when all we will be able to do is to remember that we ought to be praying more than we are.

What follows is a description of what I have called the Prayer of Stillness. This is a way of praying that I developed myself some years ago and which others have found helpful. It is similar to a form of Ignatian prayer, although I was ignorant of this when I developed it. This particular kind of prayer is not for those who cannot be still. It is for those who, for a while, want to stop rushing around meeting endless demands, and who find spiritual nourishment through sitting in silence and stillness.

You can pray this Prayer of Stillness every day although, if you were to, I would suggest that you give yourself a day 'off' each week. This is important so that we do not become spiritually stale or even exhausted by using only one form of prayer. But we might also use this prayer less often, say a couple of times a week or once a fortnight or once a month. What matters is that we do not force this Prayer of Stillness on ourselves, but rather work out where in the rhythm of our lives we can make the most of it.

This method of praying can be learned in stages. If we are pushed for time, we can still pray the first stage, say, without going on to the second. Also, if for any reason we have not prayed for a while, once the technique has been learned, it is very easy to relearn it.

I do know of those who have found this to be a very profound source of prayer and a way to 'sense' the presence of Christ. For others, it may not help at all. I can only say I hope that those who can pray in this way will find it to be a continual source of joy and blessing.

16

The five stages of the Prayer of Stillness

———◆◆◆———

What follows is simply a help to being still in the presence of God, using a prayer of attentiveness, Bible imagery and imagination. Five stages are outlined, together with additional comments on how to get used to this way of praying, and some final words of encouragement.

Stage 1: Settling down to pray

- Find a time to be quiet when you won't be disturbed. Try and sort the phone out so that if it rings, it will not distract you. If others are around you, ask them to be sensitive to your need for silence. Try and set aside 40 minutes. You may not need all this time, but, on the other hand, sometimes you may need a little more.

- Choose somewhere where you can pray. Some places at home are better than others. Try to find somewhere where there is as little as possible to distract you. Some areas of the house at certain times of the day have a particular atmosphere of calm. There is no 'right' place or 'wrong' place. Make your choice based on what feels best for you.

- Posture is important so that the position of your body helps rather than hinders your prayer. If, say, after ten minutes you find you have backache, the discomfort from this may distract you. Where you decide to sit is important. For this kind of prayer, it is recommended that you use a chair which enables you to sit with your bottom pushed to the back of the seat, with good support for your back which itself should be as straight as possible. It is good to make yourself as comfortable as you can so that once you have settled into prayer, you don't fidget!

  Now place your feet flat on the floor and sit with them uncrossed. Place your hands gently on your thighs. You can place them either palms down or up depending upon which you find more helpful and effective in prayer. As time goes on, you will discover which way is best for you. Some people find that if they are opening themselves up to God, or if they are putting themselves in 'receiving' mode, it is more appropriate to sit with their hands palms up. Once again, there are no hard and fast rules. Make your decision based on what feels most natural or comfortable for you.

  At this point, sit 'proud' with your head slightly tilted up as if you are gently gazing up into heaven. As you progress through this time of prayer, you may find that your head drops down so that your chin rests on your chest. This is fine and can be a natural result of your praying.

  By the way, don't worry about falling asleep! Much of this particular way of praying depends upon your being relaxed.

The more relaxed you are, the better. So if you are tired, it is quite likely you may fall asleep. Deep prayer is like deep sleep. God can still minister to us while we sleep. However, if you do fall asleep regularly then maybe you need to find a different time of day or night to pray, or perhaps you need some early nights to catch up on your sleep!

- At this point become conscious of your breathing and, initially, try to slow it down a little. We will return to this later but for now try to breathe from the depths of your stomach (diaphragm) rather than from your throat or chest. Breathe in and out using as much air as possible to fill your lungs and exhale. To begin with, you could spend several minutes – or as long as it takes – to regulate your breathing so that it becomes deeper. If you find this difficult for medical reasons, do what you can and don't worry. Being short of breath will not prevent you from praying deeply. Just try to breathe as naturally as you can.

- In order to ease the tension out of your body, close your eyes and tense all your muscles or at least as many as you can. Begin by curling your toes and tensing your calf muscles, work through your body and end by frowning and tightening the muscles in your forehead. Hold yourself like this for a short while and gradually release the tension from each muscle group, letting them release as much as you can before starting again with your toes and working through to the top of your head. You can make up your own prayers to say for different parts of your body as you relax them, such as:

> 'Lord, help me to use my feet carefully, knowing that I walk on holy ground.'

> 'Lord, make my legs strong so that when I need to, I can walk against the tide of godlessness.'

> 'Lord, fill my sexual parts with love and goodness.'

> 'Lord, let my inward parts help my service of you.'

> 'Lord, make my back upright and strong that I may stand up for you.'

> 'Lord, use my hands to welcome and help others.'

'Lord, come into my mind and think through it, come into my eyes and see through them, come into my mouth and speak through it, come into my heart and love through it. Amen.'

Repeat this tensing and untensing of your muscles as many times as it takes in order for you to be able to relax fully into God's presence. This may take a minute, several minutes or longer.

Stage 2: Settling in to pray

You should at this point be feeling physically very still. It is now time to concentrate further on your breathing. What follows is an approach which you may find suits you perfectly. But if it doesn't, adapt it to suit yourself while retaining the basic structure. However, before you begin this section, select a scene from the Gospels which, having Jesus as its central figure, you can picture or imagine in your mind in detail. You will need this picture later on so, when you have made your selection, file it at the back of your mind where you can easily retrieve it.

Now, back to your breathing:

- Listen first to the way you are breathing at present and the rate at which you are breathing. Having focused in this way, begin to breathe more deeply, at the same time slowing down your rate. Remember to breathe from your diaphragm (stomach area) rather than from your chest. Allow your stomach muscles to relax as you breathe in, so that your abdomen looks like a pair of bellows filling with air. Breathe in through your nose and out through your mouth. Try not to rush this. Take your time and feel yourself relaxing more and more. In order to regulate your breathing as effectively as possible, count slowly from 1 to 6 in your mind when you are breathing in. (If you can't manage to get to 6 then count as long as it takes to fill your lungs very slowly.) Similarly, as you breathe out, count slowly from 1 to 6. Doing this should prevent you from accelerating your breathing rate. Repeat this for a while so that the counting is automatic and requires very little mental effort.
- The next stage is to hold your breath for a short time both when you have finished breathing in and when you have finished breathing out. Again, you are the best judge of how long you can hold your breath comfortably. If you are counting 1 to 6 when breathing in, then holding your breath for a count of up to 1 to 4 would be appropriate. You need to hold your breath as long as you can without feeling uncomfortable. Your complete breathing rhythm should now be something like this:

Breathe in: count 1 to 6
Hold breath: count 1 to 4

Breathe out: count 1 to 6
Hold breath: count 1 to 4
Breathe in: count 1 to 6
and so on.

Do not at any time force yourself to breathe in a way that is significantly uncomfortable or causes you distress in any way. Simply adapt this breathing exercise to suit you. If at any time you feel dizzy or at all unwell as a result of this breathing exercise, stop immediately and seek advice and help if appropriate.

- Now, in order to turn this breathing exercise into a deep prayer by which you welcome the Spirit of Christ into your heart, say these words (or similar words of your own choice) silently as you breathe. Try and make the words last as long as it takes to breathe in and out.

Breathing in: *Spirit of the living God, come and fill me now.*
               or
               Lord Jesus Christ, Son of the living God, fill me with your Spirit now.

Holding your
  breath: Say nothing. Wait on God.
Breathing out: *Heavenly Father, thank you.*
               or
               Thank you, Lord Jesus. Amen.

Continue with this pattern of breathing until you have settled into it and feel very relaxed and comfortable with it.

Stage 3: Drawing closer to Jesus

While you are breathing and praying as above, and while keeping your eyes closed, begin to 'look' at an imaginary blank screen just in front of your forehead and above your eyes.

You are now about to focus your prayers specifically on Jesus. IT IS IMPORTANT YOU DO NOT LOOK AT JESUS UNTIL RIGHT AT THE END OF THIS SECTION AS INDICATED. By now you have relaxed your body, regulated your breathing and engaged in a deep prayer of the spirit. While keeping your eyes closed, turn your attention to the blank screen you have imagined in front of your nose. Be aware of the screen, its size, texture and how far it reaches. On to that screen now gently place the scene from the Gospels you selected earlier. Let it settle onto the screen. Look slowly at the scene and let your gaze wander around the picture in front of you. Look at the buildings, shapes and figures *but do not look at Jesus yet.*

Look at the people, have a look at their feet and what they are wearing on them. What clothing do they have? Are they wearing anything on their heads? (There are *no* rights or wrongs here. It is not as if the prayer will malfunction if you get historical details wrong. It is important that you let your imagination go.) Now look at the people's faces in detail . . . What is their skin texture and colour like? What do their eyes look like? Now listen to what is going on, to the sounds of people's voices for example. What are they saying? Have a look at the surroundings – such as buildings or maybe countryside. What can you see?

(People have different dominant senses. One may be visual, one aural, another tactile. Some 'visualize' in terms of sounds and tactile sensation. It is all right if you feel that everything is not about seeing. In which case, you may prefer to concentrate on using your other senses. When contemplating the image that you have placed on your screen, it may be helpful to sense how hot it is. Is the air dirty? Does it smell of spices? Think about what you might 'touch' in the scene and go ahead and make contact with it. How does it feel? Is it different in any way from what you had expected?)

When you have taken in the scene as much as you can, turn your attention slowly to the figure of Jesus. *Whatever your story or scene, you need to make sure that until now, he has had his back to you.* At this point he still has his back to you. Now gradually, slowly approach him. As you do so, you will see him more clearly and hear his voice and what he is saying.

When you get to within a few feet of him imagine that he *slowly* turns around to face you. He looks straight at you, looking into your eyes, and then he says . . .

The rest is up to you . . . or more precisely is down to your spiritual 'dialogue' with Jesus. Try not to force your conversation with him. It is important that you let him talk to you and lead the conversation himself.

Stage 4: Being with Jesus

This is the place of prayer that you have been preparing yourself for – this, if you like, is the climax of this kind of prayer.

You've made it to this point and I can take you no further. I hesitate to suggest what may happen next as this may be to put thoughts into your mind or to suggest 'norms', things that are likely to happen. Suffice it to say that at this point you are at your most private and personal place of communication or, to be more precise, communion with Christ. Just simply go with it . . . Or rather, go with him wherever he takes you. Listen carefully to what he says to you. Again, you don't have to 'do' anything, just be yourself.

This stage may last seconds or a minute or a few minutes or half an hour or longer. There are no time limits, although you will probably be aware when it is right for this communion to come to an end. The precise time this stage takes does not necessarily determine the effectiveness of your communion with Christ. Just stay here as long as is appropriate and enjoy/delight in this prayer. The effectiveness will have more to do with the nature of the communion that takes place than with the specific time you give to this.

Stage 5: Being with the world again

When you feel this stage has finished, or you want to end your time of prayer, try and 'come back' gradually. Take your time. You have been a long way since you first sat down. You will not have moved for a while and, for the most part, you will have been unaware of your surroundings.

To 'come back' you might begin by gently moving your toes and feet and work up your body. Move your fingers and your hands slowly. They may feel a little heavy to begin with. Move your head from side to side and stretch your neck as you open your eyes slowly and begin to look around and take in the room in which you have been.

Now is the time to make a note of anything in your time of prayer you want to retain for further thought or action. You may want to keep a prayer diary or more specifically keep a record of what happened when you met Jesus. You may want to make a note of a question(s) or idea(s) that you wish to pursue. (Try not to make notes as you pray as this can be very distracting while you are engaged in this particular method of praying. Always try and wait until you have finished.)

When you have done this, sit for a short while in thankfulness to God for your time of prayer. When the time is right, stand up slowly. As you get to your feet, you might feel the need to hold on to the chair to steady yourself. Begin by taking a few small steps as you begin to move around again.

You may like to make the sign of the cross or make some other sign as a symbol of the ending of your set time of prayer and as a reminder that you are moving from a particular time of prayer into the prayer of your life.

Some additional comments on how to get used to this way of praying

- If this is a different way of prayer for you, you might find it easier to get used to it a stage at a time. You will need to have repeated the procedure a sufficient number of times before you can go through it without referring to these notes or wondering what to do next.
- If you would find it helpful, I suggest that to begin with you spend the quiet time of prayer you have set aside simply going through the first two stages until you feel very comfortable with them and can go through them without any problems.
- Always remember that in the first two stages you are praying. Sitting still in the presence of God and focusing on him *is* prayer. The prayers of breathing *are* prayers. So if you don't have the time on any one occasion to get beyond the first two stages, don't worry. You haven't wasted your time. You've actually been praying and you will notice the benefit afterwards of having opened yourself up to God in prayer like this.
- If, not having prayed like this for a while, you want to return to it and make it again a central part of your prayer life, then begin from the beginning. In other words, practise the first two stages on their own for a while and when you are ready, go on to stages 3 and 4.
- Some people like to remain with the same picture of Jesus (Gospel story) all the time. There is nothing wrong with this. Others may feel that after a while they would like to look at a different picture of Jesus (Gospel story). Try not to change the picture because there is something in it that you need to work on but can't be bothered to come to terms with.

Final comment

We all have our favourite sayings on prayer which help us focus on what really matters. I have two in particular:

The simplicity of prayer is naked love. (Mother Mary Clare, SLG)

Pray as you can for prayer does not consist of thinking a great deal, but of loving a great deal. (St Teresa of Avila)

You might like to note down your own favourite sayings.

Notes

1 Father Matta El-Meskeen, *Orthodox Prayer Life: The Interior Way* (Crestwood, NY: St Vladimir's Seminary Press, 2003), p. 36.
2 St Isaac the Syrian who wrote in the seventh century.
3 It is interesting to note that God first reveals himself to Moses as the God of history, i.e. the God of Abraham, Isaac and Jacob. Moses is encouraged to appreciate fully the presence of God by recalling all that God has done for his people in the past.
4 Archimandrite Sophrony, *On Prayer* (Crestwood, NY: St Vladimir's Seminary Press, 1996), p. 82.
5 Archimandrite Sophrony, *On Prayer*, p. 10.
6 *Common Worship: Pastoral Services* (London, Church House Publishing, 2000; copyright © The Archbishops' Council, 2000). Permission sought from The Archbishops' Council.
7 *The Cloud of Unknowing* (Harmondsworth: Penguin Books Ltd, first published 1961), p. 106.
8 Published in accordance with the Prayer Book Measure, 1928. Extracts from The Book of Common Prayer, the rights in which are vested in the Crown, are reproduced by permission of the Crown's Patentee, Cambridge University Press.
9 From Wednesday Vigils, *Benedictine Daily Prayer: A Short Breviary*, compiled and edited by Maxwell E. Johnson, Oblate of St John's Abbey, and the Monks of St John's Abbey (Dublin: Columba Press, 2005), p. 1053.
10 From Friday Vigils, *Benedictine Daily Prayer: A Short Breviary*, p. 1105.
11 From Night Prayer (Compline), *Common Worship: Daily Prayer* (London: Church House Publishing, 2005; copyright © The Archbishops' Council, 2005), p. 346. Permission sought from The Archbishops' Council.
12 Archimandrite Sophrony, *His Life is Mine*, translated from the Russian by Rosemary Edmonds (Crestwood, NY: St Vladimir's Seminary Press, 1998; first published by A. R. Mowbray & Co Ltd, 1977), p. 62.
13 Brother Lawrence, *The Practice of the Presence of God*, translated by E. M. Blaiklock (London: Hodder and Stoughton, 1981), p. 37.
14 John O'Donohue, *Eternal Echoes* (London: Bantam Books, 2000), p. 164.
15 John Main, *Moment of Christ* (London: Darton, Longman and Todd Ltd, 1984), p. x.

16 Fyodor Dostoyevsky, *The Brothers Karamazov* (Harmondsworth: Penguin Books Ltd, 1982), p. 376.

17 Prayer E, *Common Worship* (London: Church House Publishing, 2000; copyright © The Archbishops' Council, 2000), p. 197. Permission sought from The Archbishops' Council.

18 St Augustine, *Confessions*, Book iv, Ch. 12 (Harmondsworth: Penguin Books Ltd, 1961), p. 82.

19 She uses the words, 'Lord' which may represent a Gentile's approach to Jesus, and also 'Son of David' which was a Hebrew title. By doing so, she could be hedging her bets, or we might see here a recognition that the kingdom of God, rather than being confined to one religion, comes into being with every expression of authentic love.

20 Evelyn Underhill, *The Spiritual Life* (Oxford: Oneworld Publications, 1993), p. 18.

21 Adapted from one of a number of prayers written by the author for use at the Lambeth Conference 2008.

22 Archimandrite Sophrony, *Words of Life* (Essex: Stavropegic Monastery of St John the Baptist, 2nd (revised) edn, 1998), p. 55.

23 With due acknowledgement to Mother Mary Clare SLG for her words, 'The simplicity of prayer is naked love'. (From *The Simplicity of Prayer*, Fairacres: SLG Press, 1988).

24 These are very simple general terms. There are, of course, many examples in the Old Testament of how faithful people try to come to terms with love and the love of God.